NO PLACE to HIDE

Wife Abuse:
Anatomy of a Private Crime

Esther Lee Olson
with Kenneth Petersen

Tyndale House Publishers, Inc., Wheaton, Illinois

*To my mother, Lillian
And the men in my life:
My father, Olaf
My husband, Hank
And my sons, Kevin and Bernard.*

Second printing, April 1983

Library of Congress Catalog Card Number 82-80967
ISBN 0-8423-4721-6
Copyright © 1982 by Esther Olson and Kenneth Petersen
All rights reserved
Printed in the United States of America

Contents

7
Introduction

11
One **Fists of Rage and Shattered Dreams**

15
Two **Claire**

23
Three **The Honeymoon Is Over**

33
Four **Peace Child?**

43
Five **The Permanent Covenant**

51
Six **The "Good" Years**

63
Seven **Saturday Scenes**

77
Eight **Promises, Promises**

87
Nine **Morning Has Broken**

101
Ten **Falling Apart into Wholeness**

113
Eleven **The Homecoming**

121
Epilogue

127
Appendix One **Christian Women and Abuse**

143
Appendix Two **Help from Books**

Acknowledgments

Many people have had a hand in preparing me for the task of writing this book. Special thanks to my sisters and brothers: to Joan and Bernard, who in death have taught me the meaning of life; and to Barb, Larry, Ken, and Bob, from whom I've learned the quality of loving relationships.

It was from Dr. Richard Dobbins, Dr. Douglas Dahlquist, and Dr. David Anderson that I learned the valuable principle of helping those who hurt. And Dottie Stevens, with unending effort, has been God's servant to me. Their quality of compassion has been invaluable.

And finally, I am most grateful for the friendship and guidance of Jerry Jenkins. His convictions about wife abuse helped bring an idea to life. His concern for me and this project was often what kept me going. And his encouragement and professional advice gave the book shape and direction.

No Place to Hide is just one part of a larger ministry to those who suffer emotionally. In Luke 4:18, Jesus says, "The Spirit of the Lord is upon me, because he hath anointed me to preach the gospel to the poor; he hath sent me to heal the brokenhearted, to preach deliverance to the captives, and recovering of sight to the blind, to set at liberty them that are bruised." It is my hope and prayer that through this ministry and this book, hurting people might encounter healing and refuge in Christ Jesus.

Esther Lee Olson

If all the men in the world
who abuse their wives
were laid end to end,
it would be a good thing.

—Charlie Shedd

Introduction

Wife abuse.

To the ignorant, wife abuse is something a wife has coming to her.

To the naive, wife abuse is a social problem which isn't desirable yet is somewhat inevitable.

To the curious, wife abuse is bizarre and occurs only in bad marriages.

To Christians, wife abuse is something that happens to non-Christians.

To most of us, wife abuse is depressing, and we'd rather not think about it.

But to the battered woman the term assaults the senses and lodges hard in the emotions. It unleashes a flood of memories, nightmares, recollections of fear and horror. It reminds her of her shattered dream of marriage; it triggers doubts about her role as a woman, her sex, her femininity. To the battered woman, "wife abuse" means more than just that she has suffered pain or that she has been scarred or, possibly, disfigured. It means something more—that attempts have been made to eradicate her identity and her very being.

What follows is the true story of a woman who was beaten by her husband hundreds of times over nearly twenty years. But it is also about those who were ignorant, naive, and curious. It is a story about Christians and religious, well-heeled, upper middle-class people, a story about pastors and doctors and lawyers, a story about the children who watched it happen. In a way, this is a story about us all.

Claire is the abused wife in this book. Charles is her husband, a batterer. Their names, the names of friends and relatives, and certain details of this account have been changed to protect those involved. In some cases incidents have been rearranged or reconstructed to meet the special demands of putting a person's life into book form. But be assured that this story is true.

No Place to Hide concerns the events of Claire's life as well as the healing that took place under the care of counselor Esther Olson. Putting it another way, we have tried to represent both the physical and psychological elements of Claire's story. It is our belief that this approach will be the most helpful to women caught in the clutches of abuse.

We need to make four things clear before we begin:

1. We have tried to make a difficult subject as palatable as possible without compromising its seriousness and horror. This hasn't been easy. We live in a time when most nonfiction books are happy stories about people who have become successful. We'd all rather escape from problems than confront them. We confess that at times, in the interest of attracting a wider readership to a most significant problem, we have been tempted to bill even this as a "success story." It does, after all, contain elements of hope within it.

But this is not a success story. And we can't make it one. Despite the fact that Claire is now living with her husband and that the marriage has been "preserved," there remain deep wounds and great pain. Everything is *not* "all better." We trust you will not be tempted, as we were, to put a happy face on a sad story.

We promise this: we will be careful with your emotions. The details of the physical abuse will be represented, but carefully, and never will we be more graphic than is necessary.

2. Claire should not be taken as a model for abused wives. There is a lot we can learn from Claire, but in most cases she offers us examples of what should *not* be done rather than what should be done. Claire's case has been chosen because it is typical, not because it represents an ideal way of handling wife abuse.

Claire stayed with her husband for nearly twenty years. That may appear virtuous to some. It wasn't. It was a grave mistake. It nearly killed her.

Our advice to the abused wife is this: Get professional help immediately and, if need be, leave the home and protect yourself. Once the abuse is established in a chronic pattern, it won't get better. This advice is explained in more detail later in the book. It is not given rashly, but has been carefully considered and has at heart the welfare and healing of all the parties involved.

3. *Wife abuse is not rare.* The statistics are mind-boggling: One of every two wives in America has been abused by her husband. Four to five million have been badly hurt. Millions are regularly beaten and are seemingly unaware of or afraid to take advantage of opportunities for protection, counseling, and legal recourse. Shelters for abused women, the few available, are jammed.

4. *Sad to say, wife abuse occurs in Christian homes too.* A sociological study conducted by Straus, Gelles, and Steinmetz in 1976 found that battered women come from all religious backgrounds, that many have strong, deep beliefs in God, and that the majority come from "middle-class and higher-income homes where the power of their wealth is in the hands of their husbands."

Indeed, one of the purposes of this book is to address a special problem that abused Christian women face: their strong doctrinal adherence to a biblical concept of marriage and submission. It is important here to state the fact that the authors of this book are born-again Christians. We are concerned, however, that some Christian teachings, taken to extremes, yield highly dangerous situations for Christian women who are being abused. Claire's is a case in point: her religious background, her strong faith, her belief in biblical submission, and her intense conviction to save her marriage nearly cost her her life. We think that the sanctity of life, in such a case, ought to be the predominant concern for women. But more about that later.

Maybe you picked up *No Place to Hide* because you know or suspect that a friend or relative is being abused. Perhaps you are a victim yourself. Most likely, you are reading this book out of curiosity, concerned about a problem that you have heard pervades our society.

Whatever the case, this book is for you. Claire's story offers hope and encouragement for victims of wife abuse. And the analytic eye of counselor Esther Olson puts the story into psychological and sociological perspective for those who want to know more about the problem. Above all, for any woman who is oppressed and hurting, this book seeks to offer spiritual comfort. Jesus cared about women. You can tell it by the way in which he spoke to them individually. In his conversations with the woman at the well, Mary Magdalene, Mary and Martha, and others, his tenderness and love shine through. The authors of *No Place to Hide* have, for this reason, included Jesus' words to various women at the beginnings of the chapters. Not all of these verses pertain specifically to the problem of wife abuse; not all of them relate to the story you are about to read. But they do remind us of Christ's compassion for the women of his time, a striking contrast to the violence that reigns between many men and women today.

We ask that as you read *No Place to Hide* you pray with us that the practice of wife abuse might be controlled and that God will heal those who have endured so much for so long.

> Woman, why are you weeping?
> *Jesus, to Mary Magdalene*
> *(John 20:15, RSV)*

One
Fists of Rage
and Shattered Dreams

Claire's head snapped back from the blow of her husband's fist and slammed against the kitchen cabinets. Her eyes widened with terror, and she trembled.

Charles had stormed in swearing and yelling. Rage was in his eyes, born of a dark void in him that Claire didn't understand. Breathing hard and sweating profusely, Charles had grabbed Claire's upper arm and swung her around, reeling her hard against the refrigerator. He bellied into her there, all 200 pounds of him, and Claire felt the refrigerator door handle dig painfully into her side....

This Saturday morning had given no hints of what was to happen. In fact, it had begun pleasurably, with a light breakfast and coffee on the porch. Claire and Charles had talked together—nothing but light conversation, but it had been civil conversation, as much as you could expect on a lazy Saturday morning.

But later the car wouldn't start. Charles was irritated. The hood of the Buick went up at nine o'clock; Charles plunged right in, examining the spark plugs, then taking apart the distributor. Claire had started to wash the dishes that had piled up from the party the night before. But she was tense. Once, she caught herself washing a cup four times; her mind wasn't on her work.

Outside, Charles kicked the car. He swore and banged his fist down on the fender.

Claire felt her stomach knot up. Her throat was dry. Her head pounded. She felt nauseated. She knew what was coming. She had seen it before.

Charles wasn't having much luck. It was now ten-thirty. The distributor lay in parts atop the carburetor; the spark plugs were out and the spark plug wires were dangling every which way. He had tried everything he knew how to do. They had no extra money to pay a mechanic. Charles paced around the Buick, fuming. He decided to put it all back together once again. Maybe something would fall into place.

Claire, meanwhile, had started to scrub the pans, her mind in a whirl. How could it have gone wrong? *It must be me.* Claire thought. *I must not be measuring up.*

Claire thought about how she had felt before she had been married. She remembered her adolescent dreams: a nice suburban house with trees and a yard, decorating and setting up a home, entertaining neighbors at parties and barbecues, and above all, just being with Charles on quiet summer evenings. Was it too much to ask? *I must try harder,* Claire thought.

Charles's hand slipped on the socket wrench as he was screwing a spark plug into place; his hand jammed into the side of the engine block. He swore loudly, pulled his hand back, flung the wrench wildly at the carburetor so that it made an ugly clank, kicked the front grille, and stomped toward the front door.

Inside, Claire flinched. She dropped the frying pan into the sink and whirled completely around as Charles headed for her. . . .

In real time it lasted three minutes. To Claire, in psychological time, it seemed like a hour. The first half had been loud and painful. She had screamed; Charles had yelled and grunted. The blows to her chest and stomach had caused excruciating pain. The second half of the beating was eerily silent—except for Claire gulping for air and Charles breathing fast, short breaths.

It ended as quickly as it had begun. Charles stumbled out of the kitchen, leaving Claire sobbing in a heap at the base of the refrigerator. Her knees were scraped, her nose was bleeding, and a purplish bruise was appearing on her left knee. Later large welts and bruises would appear on her chest and abdomen. There would be no accounting, however, of emotional injuries, or of the dreams that were blown apart by Charles's fists of rage.

Charles returned in fifteen minutes to ask forgiveness. He was crying. He pleaded with Claire not to say anything about the incident to neighbors or relatives. He said it would never happen again. They would start all over, he said.

Charles and Claire had been married exactly two weeks.

> You are anxious and
> troubled about many
> things.
> *Jesus, to Martha, the sister
> of Mary
> (Luke 10:41, RSV)*

Two
Claire

At the age of thirty-five, some eighteen years after she had been married, Claire had been referred to me by a physician in Fargo, North Dakota, who had, with her permission, briefed me on her case.

He told me she was depressed and apparently a victim of wife abuse. At this point the extent of the abuse wasn't known.

Claire was a farm insurance representative with a small Midwestern firm. She had worked her way up through the ranks over the years, first picking up odd jobs as a typist and secretary; then later, after she had acquired a college education, Claire had been promoted to office manager. Now as an insurance rep, she had numerous opportunities to travel. Charles, her husband, was principal of a large school. The couple had three children. Charles and Claire were socially prominent and active in the community (one of the reasons Claire traveled out of town to visit me). Also, Claire was a regular church attender and took the children to Sunday school nearly every week. Charles attended only occasionally.

The only other thing I knew was that months before Claire had moved out on Charles, lived away from home for about two months, and then moved back in. According to the physician who briefed me, all physical abuse had apparently stopped upon Claire's return home.

As she sat in my office, the only evidence of Claire's pain was a certain stiffness, a rigidity in her petite body. This attractive, dark-haired woman seemed to smile easily, but her eyes betrayed her. They never seemed to match her social grace, the way she managed herself in front of me. Claire fought to maintain eye contact, but she couldn't for long.

We set up a schedule: Claire would visit twice a month; our sessions would be three to four hours each time. Our aim would be twofold: First, to make sure the abuse would not start up again. Second, to rebuild Claire's sense of self-worth and identity, to repair her shattered personality, and to help her overcome depression and the acute anxiety she felt nearly all the time.

Before we started, I had little idea of all that Claire had been through. I was soon to find out.

Sometimes psychological counseling becomes a kind of detective work. Sometimes the pieces fall neatly into place, and motivations for certain behavior are recognizable. But often, the puzzle is not so easily solved. Wife abuse cases are like that: Why does *anyone* want to violently abuse someone else? Moreover, why does a husband, presumably bonded in love to his wife, beat her?

Claire's case was even more disturbing. She had come from a fine home. In fact, I ran into so few clients like Claire, people who grew up in close, God-conscious families where security and love are the trademarks, that time and time again I found it to be a joy just to hear her reminisce about her childhood.

Claire had been born in a Minot, North Dakota, farmhouse on the last and coldest day of 1945. Her mother had hoped to make it the less than thirty miles down old Route 52 to the hospital at Bergen, but the Chevy truck wouldn't start in below-zero weather. Husband Frederick played midwife.

Claire was the first of four children. She took seriously her role as eldest; she was the peacemaker, the diligent one, the mature one. Claire's was a big, loud, loving, affectionate family with a quiet, spiritual mother and a gregarious father who loved to wrestle with his children—all at once.

Her mom and dad cared for each other deeply and let it

show. Frederick was not ashamed to drive to church with one arm around his wife or with his hand on her knee. Claire's parents would tell me later, "We were brought up to believe that it was more of a sin to divorce than to do anything else. ... That's what was instilled in us at church. Separation was just as bad. Unheard of."

It was clear that Claire had grown up in a conservative, religious home. Her parents had held marriage in high esteem. All this, coupled with her Midwestern heritage, made young Claire the perfect image of the all-American girl.

So why was this woman sitting in my office like a psychological cliché, twisting her hankie in knotted fists, speaking vaguely and quickly, as if on the verge of tears?

By now I realized that Claire's case would take more than listening and caring. As significant as that would be, there was a puzzle here that demanded solutions. I would have to be something of a psychological detective; I would have to talk with some of the characters who played a part in this tragedy. Above all, I would have to find the answers to two important questions: *How did this happen?* and *Why did this happen to Claire?*

Mrs. Olson: How does your family compare with the one in which you grew up?
Claire: There's no comparison. We're city people. Charles is principal of the high school. I sell insurance. Mike is in high school, Debbie is in junior high, and Tricia is a fourth-grader.
Mrs. Olson: Happy?
Claire: The kids? Yes.
Mrs. Olson: You?
Claire: No. (Pause.) I left Charles once. I took all I could take, and then I left him. I knew it was the right thing to do, the thing I should have done long ago, and I felt so free. But I went back. Now I have to stay with him and I don't want to. I don't want to....
Mrs. Olson: (After a pause.) Claire, I want you to listen to me closely. I can't tell you to leave Charles or to stay with him—that's for you to decide.
Claire: (Holding a handkerchief to her eyes, nods.)

Mrs. Olson: But in the short time that we've talked together I can tell that your problem isn't the future but the past. You haven't come to terms with the past. . . . It will be painful, difficult. But it's important for you to face what has happened; you've got to deal with your guilt and anger. . . . Claire, I want you to tell me everything. You need to talk it out.
Claire: You want me to tell you my story.
Mrs. Olson: Yes, but it's more than a story. And it's not a dream, a nightmare—it's your life.
Claire: (Looking down into the floor.) Yes, it is.
Mrs. Olson: There will be times when it'll be rough, Claire. You'll cry a lot. You'll get angry. But I'll be here to help you.
Claire: (Forces a smile, nods.) Where do we start?
Mrs. Olson: Suppose you tell me about your wedding.

It was April 1960, and Charles and Claire knelt at a rickety wooden altar in a small, modest sanctuary. A minister dressed in a white robe stood before them. "Charles, do you take this woman to be your lawful wedded wife?" The minister's voice echoed against the brick walls of the church.

Claire hardly heard Charles's reply. Despite everything, all would be well. After months of family troubles, things would be OK. Yes, of course, Claire knew the hurt feelings they had left behind: her mother-in-law would be furious that the couple had eloped. But everyone would get over it, in time. And she and Charles would be man and wife. Claire looked down at the bouquet of daisies and carnations that she held in her hand. Charles had stopped along the way for them and had looked so nervous walking to and from the car. Claire caught the fresh fragrance of the flowers and smiled.

She and Charles had met while she was still in high school. He had been studying at a local community college and dating a friend of hers. As a senior, Claire found herself in a number of group dating situations with college guys. Charles and Claire first saw each other at a bowling party, but they were with other dates. Claire found out from a friend that Charles didn't date much, that he was quiet, but nice.

"He was also good-looking," Claire says of those early days

together. "The only thing about him that I remember as being aggressive was when he told me that he wanted to be called Charles, not Chuck or Charlie. I liked him. We were soon dating each other exclusively."

Charles was embarrassed about his home and family. He was the only child of elderly parents. His mother was crabby, hostile, and used coarse language with her son, even when he brought guests home. He had been reluctant to take Claire home with him, and when he finally did, she knew why.

Claire was immediately sensitive to Charles and the problems he had had growing up. She pitied him because of his strange upbringing by these people old enough to be his grandparents.

Charles's father was a silent, passive type; the mother ran the show. She had no friends; the neighbors couldn't stand her. She was jealous of her son's girl friend, and she was sometimes likely to be violent.

Claire never knew if Charles had been beaten as a child, but she had heard stories of his mother chasing people from the house with a broom.

Still, Charles rarely spoke ill of his mother, always insisting that he loved her and that she loved him, though their relationship was stormy.

Mrs. Olson: How did Charles treat you at that time?
Claire: Like a million dollars.... But he was always so jealous. One night a girl friend and I went to the fair together. Charles was supposed to be studying. (He had always wanted to be a teacher, and he was diligent in school.) But he showed up at the fair. I didn't make a big deal of it, but it bothered me. I mean, he was even jealous of my *girl* friends.

Claire became determined to show Charles a better life. She was convinced that whatever problems he had probably derived from his home life and were solvable. In view of later events this proved ironic: Claire felt that she could take care of Charles and show him that he didn't have to live with constant abuse.

After three months of dating, their relationship grew much

more serious than Claire had anticipated. Charles's jealousy became more and more obsessive. Claire spoke up about it. "I told him clearly that besides the fact he didn't have to worry about me—because I was interested in no one else—I felt he was imposing upon me and my time. I needed girl friends. I needed to be able to talk with them and do things with them, and I didn't want to have to look over my shoulder every time I talked to another guy, either."

But Charles became more possessive—and more serious. He began playing on Claire's emotions. He told her that if she didn't marry him soon, it would prove she didn't love him. And, he said, he would kill himself if he couldn't have her.

Mrs. Olson: How did you feel about that?
Claire: It scared me. I mean, I didn't know what he'd do. It was like a threat—marry me or else. Or else what? Kill himself? Esther, when I think about it... I don't know. How close I came to breaking it— (She pauses.) To breaking it off... I don't know. Well, it woke me up. He was pushing me farther than I wanted to go. I was so young and naive in those days. I know how ridiculous this sounds, but at that time I didn't even know how girls got pregnant....

Claire soon decided that she didn't want to marry Charles. She suggested on the phone that they stop seeing each other. Charles drove right over and demanded to get things straightened out.

They did—in a way.

Around this time, Charles's mother laid down an ultimatum: If Charles continued to see Claire, she would disown him and throw him out. And at one point, Charles's mother sent a registered letter to Claire's parents, threatening to sign him up for the armed forces if he didn't break up with their daughter.

The combination of oppressive mother and pitiful son began to get to Claire. Her feelings of compassion and sensitivity toward Charles began to come out. Charles and Claire became a little more comfortable with each other, partly because she was teaming up with Charles against his cruel mother. With the idea that she somehow would be able to "save" Charles from his past, Claire gradually came to think, *We might as well get married.*

That's not reason enough, Claire knows now. But it was all Charles needed to hear. She wasn't so happy about the marriage as much as she was resigned to it. He wasn't going to leave her alone, so he had won. He had conquered her. He had worn her down. She had been pushed into marrying him.

Claire's family was against the marriage. Charles had been nothing but the perfect gentleman to them, but they were very much aware that his values were the opposite of theirs. He went to church only for Claire, and no one knew how long that would last. She was a born-again Christian. He made no such claim.

The problems were just beginning. Charles's mother insisted that the couple be married in a church of her denomination, despite the fact that church didn't mean much to her —she and her husband weren't regular churchgoers, by any means. Claire, of course, wanted the marriage in her own church, but when that seemed out of the question, she chose a neutral site, a beautiful little chapel in the woods. Once again, Charles's mother objected.

On the spur of the moment, frustrated and desperate, Charles and Claire eloped, careful only to have the wedding in the right church.

Claire was just seventeen at the time.

No matter how ambivalent Claire had been about getting married, as the time approached, her excitement grew and her hopes were high. When she walked down the aisle of that simple country church, wearing a modest and lovely white dress and carrying her bouquet of yellow and white flowers, she was radiant with the promise of a new life.

"I now pronounce you, Charles and Claire, man and wife," the minister concluded. His voice, mellow, deep, and rich, rang through the sanctuary with authority.

Claire turned to Charles. They embraced and kissed. Charles's eyes sparkled with joy. They hugged again. *Things will be just fine,* Claire thought to herself. *They'll work out just fine.*

> She has wet my feet
> with her tears....
> *Jesus, speaking of the woman
> who annointed his feet
> with oil.*
> (Luke 7:44, RSV)

Three
The Honeymoon Is Over

Claire's was not the first case of wife abuse I had encountered. A psychotherapist becomes accustomed to accounts of battering and violence in the home—it pops up often, even in the case histories of people who seek counsel for unrelated problems. I had counseled dozens of abused women. I knew the problem was widespread.

One of two American women is abused to some degree. This works out to roughly 25 to 30 million women. Of these, 4.7 million are *badly* battered. Dr. Richard J. Gelles, a sociologist who has studied wife abuse extensively, makes this startling statement: "If you're going to be killed in America, it's more likely to happen by someone in your own family."

Wife abuse is not a new problem. In fact, it has a long and depressing history. It may be a more pervasive problem in our society than it used to be, and it may be that we are more aware of the problem today than ever before. But it's always been true that husbands have abused their wives. Langley and Levy, in their book *Wife Beating: The Silent Crisis*, write, "The classic cartoon of the caveman dragging a woman off by the hair depicts a scene that is anthropologically correct." Susan Brownmiller, in a concise review of medieval English common law in her book *Against Our Will: Men, Women, and Rape*, says that "the Middle Ages was a time of savage wife beating." In fact, up until the present day, it has been assumed by otherwise civilized societies that abuse was something that had to be simply endured by a wife: "Indeed it would seem that in the 19th century women were brought up in the belief that a larger license should be allowed to their husbands than to themselves and that it was the destiny of a wife to bear with as much fortitude as she could muster all but the most extreme acts of oppression by her lord and master."

But how did all of this relate to Claire? In a sense, it didn't—she wasn't just a statistic or some anonymous figure swept away by the tide of history. Claire was an individual woman, deeply troubled, who found herself in a most difficult situation. Still, it helped to keep in mind that Claire's was not just a psychological or marital problem—it was sociological and historical as well.

Already I had picked up two important clues from Claire. The first was the feeling, derived from certain things she had said about the courtship and marriage, that she blamed herself for the abuse. I wondered if she felt that she had failed to be a good, successful wife. Eventually we would have to deal with that. And knowing that wife abuse was not unique to her marriage—that the fact of battered wives was sad but true in our social history—would indeed become important to her understanding of herself.

The second clue concerned Charles. I was intrigued, though not surprised, to hear that he had shown an intense jealousy of Claire's girl friends. I would expect Charles's jealousy to become an important part of the story later on. It is a well-established pattern in such cases.

Mrs. Olson: Why did you marry him, Claire?
Claire: I felt bound to him. He wouldn't leave me alone. You know, I was touched that he seemed to care for me so much. At least that's what it seemed at the time. For some reason, I felt there was no way out of marrying him. And, you know, I've told him that. I still do tell him that.
Mrs. Olson: Tell him what?
Claire: That I married him because I felt sorry for him and felt that I had to.

Mrs. Olson: Were there any feelings at any time during your engagement when you were happy about it? Like, I'm engaged and I'm thrilled and this is my love, my future, my life?
Claire: Oh, yes. There were times when I really cared for him. It's hard, now, to think about that—to remember how I felt. But the details of the—well, certain details are real clear.
Mrs. Olson: And you must have had girl friends who were happy for you and excited about your marriage.
Claire: Sure. Until we ran off and got married, and the dresses they made for the ceremony were useless. I didn't score too many points with that one.
Mrs. Olson: Tell me about those first weeks with Charles.

The first week, everything had worked out beautifully for Charles and Claire. It had been a simple, lovely honeymoon. Charles had been at ease, warm and tender, gallant. Claire had been happy, convinced that they had done the right thing. The end had justified the means. They were happy. The pressures were off.

Even returning home and visiting Claire's parents, who, quite understandably, had been disappointed they had been left out of the wedding plans—even this had worked out well. Claire's mother and father were quick to forgive. They wished the couple the very best. In fact, they were encouraged by the way that Charles had treated Claire and that he had promised to go to church with her regularly.

The newlyweds had acquired a small country house. It was small and needed work, but it was quiet and remote. There were no neighbors very close by. They would have solitude and privacy.

On their way to their new home, on a Saturday, Claire and Charles stopped in to see his parents—to try to patch things up, especially with Charles's mother. This turned out badly.

Charles's mother had previously made it quite clear that she never wanted to see Claire again and that Claire was never ever to set foot in their (his parents') house again. When Charles and Claire arrived, he begged her to come in with him. Claire refused. She wasn't trying to be mean. She just believed that Charles's mother had meant what she had said before. Claire was trying to honor her wishes. Claire wanted Charles to get the visit over with and to get on to their new home.

But every few minutes Charles bounded out the front door and begged Claire to come in. "It's OK," he said. "She's not mad anymore. She's got a gift for us."

Claire didn't think this was very likely. She refused. Perhaps she was being a trifle obstinate by now, but she wanted to be sure she was wanted. Claire had to make sure that Charles wasn't forcing what could be a very bad scene.

Charles was livid. "You'd better come in," he hissed, "and I mean it!"

"I'm sorry," Claire replied, startled by his anger. "Maybe another day. Your mother's warning is too fresh in my mind."

He gave her a look that wouldn't have given him away as a new bridegroom, then rushed inside to tell his mother. When he returned, he was in no mood to talk. Claire tried to humor him, but he was still mad. She decided that maybe he had some right to be upset, so she let the whole thing be. She figured that it would blow over, Charles would forgive her and understand, and everything would be all right again.

Mrs. Olson: But it didn't blow over?
Claire: Hardly. I mean, I was young—just out of high school. What did I know about how long a man should stay mad? He pulls into the driveway of our little house in the middle of nowhere and as he's turning off the engine, he says, "I can't believe you wouldn't come into my parents' house! . . ."

"Well, Charles," Claire said, "I'm sorry. I just—"

Before she could finish, Charles was up, out, around the car, and at her door. Claire started to open her door, but Charles reached in and grabbed her by the arm, yanking her out. "Charles!" Claire screamed, but didn't know what else to say. She couldn't believe this was happening.

He kept a tight grip on her arm, unlocked the door of the house, and flung her into the living room. Claire was crying now, stunned by behavior she'd never before encountered. Charles's face was red and his eyes were wild. He swore at her. He said she had humiliated his mother.

Claire was afraid by now of the power Charles had over her. So far, he hadn't hurt her so much physically as emotionally. But the terrifying thing to Claire was the realization and threat of the physical advantage Charles had.

"Charles," Claire said, sobbing, "please."

He didn't want to hear anything. As he continued yelling, he rushed at her and shoved her with both hands. Claire went flying, realizing in horror that here she was a grown woman and he had pushed her right off her feet.

She landed with a thud against the arm of the couch, flipped over, and fell back on her head into the cushions. Sprawled that way, draped over the edge of the couch, she felt so vulnerable. Claire screamed and jumped up, stumbling until she found her footing.

But it was already over. Charles was sitting, his head in his hands. Later he apologized. He cried. He was terribly ashamed. Claire wanted to ask him what in the world had gotten into him, where the rage had come from. She had dated him for so long; now this. It was hard to believe it had just happened like that, with no warning. But Charles was so remorseful that Claire didn't demand any explanation. She figured what was done was done. Charles begged her forgiveness and swore he would never do it again. He also made Claire promise not to tell anyone.

He needn't have worried about Claire spreading the news around. She was ashamed. What woman would want a living soul to know that her husband had dragged her into the house and shoved her over the couch before their first week of marriage had ended? He was like a puppy the rest of the evening. They unpacked the car, tidied up the house, and went to bed.

It happened again three days later.

Claire was in the kitchen fixing dinner. Charles had had a tough day at the school (he was then vice-principal), but he seemed to relax when he got home. The car was acting up, and he decided to fiddle with it some before dinner. Claire suggested that he change his clothes first, but Charles gave her an angry "I don't want you mothering me" look, and Claire didn't say anything more.

Minutes later, she heard him swearing outside. The hood slammed down, and Charles barged into the house.

"What is it?" Claire called.

Charles swore again. "The car, what else? I don't have the money to get it fixed."

"You know, honey, I wouldn't mind taking a job somewhere to help us out with the finances. It might be good for me, you know?" Claire was trying to be helpful. It seemed a good idea. She didn't like being alone all day. But, for some reason, Claire's suggestion offended Charles.

He didn't say anything. He just backhanded her in the chest and pushed her back against the countertop. The back of Claire's head banged against the cabinets. It was then that he saw the terror in her eyes.

Again he was sorry. He didn't know why he had done it. He said he'd make it up to her. *If Claire didn't tell anyone, he'd make it up to her.*

Mrs. Olson: You didn't believe him this time, did you?
Claire: (Raising her voice indignantly.) Of course I did. I wanted so badly to believe him, to blame it all on the new house, the finances, anything.... Anyway, he cried when he apologized.
Mrs. Olson: So you thought he was sincere?
Claire: Oh, he was. I believe that. I believe he's always sincere.
Mrs. Olson: You think that when he promises never to hurt you again, he believes he never will?
Claire: Yes. Well, *I* know he can't keep the promise. It didn't take me long to learn that. But he means it with all his heart.
Mrs. Olson: So you forgave him again?
Claire: It wasn't easy this time. I was horrified. I wanted to not believe it had happened a second time. I prayed so hard and believed so deeply that this would be the last time. I actually convinced myself of it.
Mrs. Olson: But it wasn't the last time.
Claire: No.
Mrs. Olson: How long before the next incident?
Claire: Three days.
Mrs. Olson: Again?

Claire: (Her voice cracks.) Again. Three times within the first two weeks of marriage.

I was beginning to get a picture of the scope of the abuse. I wanted Claire to tell me how many times she had been beaten in her eighteen years of marriage, but I didn't want to ask that question insensitively. She was working through the early incidents, one by one. It wouldn't be necessary to examine the violence of every incident—we wouldn't have to go through the pain of recounting each occurrence. For now, though, I hoped her ability to describe those early days of marriage (less painful because they were farther back in time —eighteen years away) would lead her to tell me the full extent of the abuse. It was important for her to tell me this— to form the words with her own lips and to see the mental pictures they conjured up. This first step to self-awareness is a most essential part of therapy.

I asked Claire about the third incident, the time he bumped her with all his weight, about 200 pounds, into the refrigerator. "The door handle left a bruise on my hip that lasted for days." Claire sipped her coffee, and paused. It was hard for her to remember details that far back. "I know I made the mistake that time of trying to slap him back. I never thought I'd do that, but when I was crushed against the refrigerator, I just lashed out. I learned a lesson from that."

"Was he immediately remorseful again, as before?"

"Oh, yes. But not until after he had grabbed my wrist and twisted me to the floor. He was about to kick me when I buried my head in my arms and screamed. Then he dropped to his knees and cradled me like a baby. He cried and cried. He begged me to forgive him, but I didn't say anything. He was so pitiful. He didn't think I would accept his apology. He was like a child. He helped me up and I went into the bedroom. Our hamburgers burned in the broiler, I remember— it was a mess. He finally worked forgiveness out of me, and then wanted to have sex."

"Right then?"

"Yes, right then. I tried to make some excuse about lunch, but he insisted."

"And so did you?" I asked.

"Yes, I did. We did. I was hardly in the mood."

"How long was it before the next incident?"

"The next *beating,* you mean?" Claire was quick with the reply. It was obviously important to her.

"Is that what you want to call these episodes?" I asked her.

"Don't you?"

"Claire, I want you to tell me. Frankly, yes, I see these acts of aggression designed to hurt you or control you or dominate you as beatings. But, bad as they were, it is interesting that these incidents weren't even worse."

"So?"

"So, it might have been difficult to prosecute in a court of law, if you had so desired."

"Back then?"

"Yes."

"I wasn't prepared for that then, no. But these *are* beatings."

"I'm not disputing you, Claire."

Claire sat back in her chair. "Do you know that in eighteen years of living with Charles, I have never been hit in the face? I have had bruises around my eyes and cheekbones and I have cut my lip when my head slammed into something—he'd throw me around pretty good—but his fists never hit me in the face."

"And what do you make of that?"

"I finally decided that he can't blame it on uncontrollable rage. Rage wouldn't be so careful not to leave facial bruises."

I was glad to know Claire had understood that. "That's true enough," I said. "Has Charles tried to blame it on uncontrollable rage?"

"One of his doctors has. Charles doesn't blame it on anything. He says he could have killed me if he had wanted to, and because he never punched me in the face, he must not have wanted to."

"I can see why you want to call these incidents beatings, then."

"Yes. Because that's what they are. There was always something *intentional* about them."

"Were you ever seriously hurt, Claire?"

"Well, yes. I've had some serious back problems as a result. Sprains. Lots of cuts—scrapes and scratches. He sometimes would grab me by the shoulders and shake me until I nearly passed out. Then he would push me and kick me." Claire paused. "That's not to mention the emotional pain. That was worse."

"What do you mean?"

"It's hard to describe. I guess it's just the idea of the person you love the most trying to kill you. How does that make you feel? You get numb after a while. You have to—to endure it."

"Claire, just how long did this go on? Are you telling me that you were beaten every few days with no letup?"

"There was a break in there for a couple of years when nothing happened. For most of our eighteen years together, though, I have been beaten. For the first few years of our marriage, he beat me several times a month."

"Do you hear what you're saying?"

"Absolutely," Claire replied. Her face was grim and her eyes were watery with tears. "You don't forget something like this."

> Jesus touched her hand, and the fever left her. . . . This was to fulfill what was spoken by the prophet Isaiah, 'He took our infirmities and bore our diseases.'
> *At the healing of Peter's mother-in-law (Matt. 8:15, 17, RSV)*

Four
Peace Child?

In my counseling of abused women, I had become amazed by the fact that these women not only seemed to take the abuse, but they also somehow felt responsible for it. There were traces of that in Claire.

She seemed to feel it was her responsibility to try to keep things on an even keel. *She* would keep Charles cool. *She* wouldn't agitate him. *She* would do whatever she could to keep him from losing control. And when he wanted forgiveness, he got it. It was as if the problem were hers, not his.

What was it about this phenomenon, which Jennifer Baker Fleming, founder and director of The Women's Resource Network, calls "a national pastime," that makes the victim see herself as the guilty party?

In her book, *Stopping Wife Abuse,* Fleming says that women must challenge the notion that "we are inherently inferior and masochistic and have a neurotic need to be abused." She continues, "The important thing to remember is that it's *your husband* who has the problem, not you. Sometimes it can be difficult to hold on to that realization, but it is absolutely necessary if you are truly to understand the situation in which you find yourself. Feeling guilty will only serve to misdirect your energy and perpetuate the violence."

Claire's biggest problem, it seemed to me, was that she was under the delusion—or had been for the first several years—that the abuse would go away by itself. She would "do better," or Charles would mature, or financial burdens would lighten, or whatever.

On that score, I was glad Claire was so insistent on convincing me she was a beaten wife, though her initial physical injuries were not as severe as some women whose husbands beat them with baseball bats or their fists until they are unconscious. But she had been *beaten*—Claire was adamant about that—and facing that fact was the second step toward help, healing, and recovery. Claire's first step had been taken when she climbed into the car to come visit me. (Abused women need to realize how important it is to have some outside opinion—even if it isn't a professional, but just a friend or relative.)

Every wife abuse case represents two psychological mysteries, embodied in a husband and a wife. Why does a husband beat his wife? Why does his wife take it? These are always the first two questions. In Claire's case, the second question became the most intriguing. While it is true that most abused women stay with their husbands longer than they should, it is rare to find an abuse case that has lasted eighteen years. Claire had stayed with Charles for a long, long time, despite continuous beatings. Why?

In those first months of marriage Claire had been beaten numerous times, yet her hope never died that somehow it would all come to an end and everything would be better. But Claire had nowhere to turn. Charles had threatened to kill her if she told anyone.

From time to time she was able to spend a day at a girl friend's house in town. This was good for her because the country place was so lonely and depressing. Despite these occasional visits, Claire never told her girl friend about the beatings. In fact, it was a long, long time before *anyone* knew about the problem.

Charles was bothered by these visits in town. Claire thought at first that he was jealous of her girl friend or her girl friend's husband (even though he was twice Claire's age). Later she realized that Charles was just worried that someone might find out what he was doing to her.

By now, Claire had learned to read Charles's moods. She could tell by the look on his face when the rage was getting hold of him. He would swear. He'd slam doors and throw objects around. Soon Claire just became something else to throw, although more often than not it started with Charles punching and shoving her. Claire would beg, "Please, please don't," but that had the effect of encouraging him. In later years he would go berserk—yet there was always something planned about the attacks. Claire noticed that he'd rip out the phone or park his car behind hers *before* he would "go crazy."

Within a year Claire was pregnant. The beatings didn't stop.

It didn't surprise me to hear this. Case studies show that women are often abused when pregnant. Sometimes the pregnancy itself serves as a trigger of the violence.

What Claire told me next seemed to verify this.

"We'd been in the country house about a year when I had had enough," Claire said to me.

That was so refreshing to hear that I had trouble suppressing a smile. Here had been a pregnant woman, in many ways still a child, who had come to the end of the line. She told Charles that he had better find them a place in town because she would move out if he didn't. She couldn't stand the isolation, the distance from the road and neighbors. She prayed that the move to a more populated section would curb the violence.

Whatever the outcome of the move, it seemed to me that this had been a significant turning point. Claire had found a weapon with which to defend herself. She learned she could threaten Charles and that it would lead to action.

Threaten him during a fight, no. But rather when he was calm, vulnerable, insecure. She would then threaten to tell someone, to move out, or to force him to get help. He pleaded his reputation in the community and with his family and friends.

It was clear to me that Claire's threats had been empty ones. Fortunately for Claire, Charles didn't realize this. Claire had no intention of moving out on Charles. She still felt deep down that somehow all of this was her fault. And then there was the issue of the sanctity of marriage. She said to me, "My church, my parents, my friends didn't believe in separation, let alone divorce. So neither did I. I was trapped." Claire thought that to move out on her husband—whatever the situation—would be terribly, terribly wrong. So when she threatened to move out, it was just talk.

Mrs. Olson: But there's something here that I still don't quite understand. What brought you to the point where you felt you could threaten him that way?
Claire: You mean, threaten to move out?
Mrs. Olson: Yes. This is the first time you actually felt capable of *doing* something about this predicament. Either you grew stronger along the way or found some other resources—
Claire: No.
Mrs. Olson: Or you became so desperate that you had to threaten him with something.
Claire: That's it.
Mrs. Olson: What made you finally talk tough?
Claire: The day Charles nearly killed me.

Claire sat silently in the passenger's seat of Charles's new royal blue Chevy. Charles was driving—and fuming. They were returning from church on a Sunday noon. Charles was angry because the sermon had gone ten minutes late. Claire, who attended church regularly, had persuaded Charles to come with her this Sunday. "There's a new man there now," she said. "He won't go beyond twelve."

There wasn't anything that Charles hated more than long sermons. To think that some preacher could keep him sitting in that pew past the allotted time. . . .

Claire had been wrong. The new man, who had been so prompt to end his sermons right at noon the previous Sundays, went overtime. Charles started to fidget at one minute past the hour. Claire could sense his rage building. At the closing prayer, Charles dragged her out of the service and pushed her into the car.

It wasn't just that. Charles had wanted roast beef for Sunday dinner. Claire said they couldn't afford roast beef—especially after Charles had committed them to ninety-dollar-a-month car payments on his new prize Chevy. They argued a while, and Charles was getting very angry. Claire saw the signs of his rage and shut up.

"Don't you think I'm good enough for a car like this, huh?" Charles said loudly. "Don't you think I deserve this?"

Claire had learned how to reply. "Of course, you do."

"I work hard for this. I've got a good job. I ought to be able to have roast beef if I want it."

"I think so, too," Claire said cautiously, "but it's just that—"

"Why do you always get in the way of what I want?" Charles was yelling now, and his eyes were burning with the fire inside him.

He grabbed her hair and yanked it. Claire yelled. Charles shoved her hard against the door. The car was all over the road. Claire thought that if she wasn't killed by Charles, she'd certainly be killed in an auto accident. She tried to calm him. "OK, OK," she said through stifled sobs. "You're right. We'll do whatever you think is best."

Within minutes they reached home. Charles's rage had not died, it was plain to Claire. Charles got out of the car and slammed the door angrily.

Claire pretended to get out too, but as soon as his back was turned, she slid over and thrust her own key into the ignition. It was a mistake. Charles heard her from the porch just as the engine was turning over. Claire locked both doors, and Charles stomped toward her, his face red and his mouth spitting out profanity. A split second before she could get the car into reverse, Charles started to kick in the window on the driver's side. And before Claire could get the car moving, Charles had bashed the window in, reached through, opened the door, and dragged Claire out onto the grass.

He pulled her over to a grove of trees to the east of their property where he nearly choked her to death. He refrained from hitting or punching, possibly because of the child within her.

Later, Claire pulled herself together and made it into the house. Charles came and begged forgiveness. Claire curtly issued her ultimatum: she would move into town, with or without him.

She moved into town. He went with her.

A month before her first child was born, Claire went with Charles for a week's vacation with his parents. Surprisingly, Claire looked forward to the week with her in-laws. Since the honeymoon, her relationship with them had improved considerably. Charles's mother had warmed to her, and the week there promised a respite from the beatings.

Early in their marriage, Charles's folks had come to visit them in the country house. It was a strange visit, because they came at night, as if on the spur of the moment. Charles was not yet home from work. They hadn't stayed long, but before they left they lifted the rifle from the wall and took it with them.

"It was chilling," Claire recalled. "It seemed that they suspected he might try to shoot me. I was ashamed."

By now, Claire had come to see Charles's mother as a friend —or at least an ally. The old woman didn't seem to know about the beatings, but she seemed now to favor Claire.

But if Claire thought the visit with her in-laws would give her time to relax, she was dead wrong. The second day there, while Charles was putting new brakes on the car, Claire heard him swearing and slamming things around. She looked out the window with her in-laws. The three of them saw Charles kick the car, nearly shoving it off the jack. He then unleashed his anger on the doghouse, beating it to pieces with a tool.

When he stormed inside, Claire hid behind the old couple, fearing for her life and the life of her unborn. Charles tried to get at her, cursing and fuming, but his own father blocked his path. "Charles, you're nothing but an SOB and you always have been. This woman is too good for you, and if she had any brains she'd leave you."

Claire was shocked by her own pity of Charles when he turned and left. It stabbed her heart to think that a man's own father would say something like that, true or not.

Claire sat and told her in-laws some, but not all, of what had been going on. "They didn't act surprised," Claire remembers. "They told me that that was why they had taken the rifle."

Claire had hoped the move into the city would be her salvation. It wasn't. The beatings continued, each time following the same pattern. Each time, afterwards, Charles would come back to her like a puppy. He'd be sorry, ashamed, and he always promised never to do it again. His promise was always attached to the condition that Claire never tell anyone.

Claire then hoped that having the baby would change her life. She looked forward to the delivery with eagerness. She would give life to the baby, and the baby would give new life to Claire. Surely Charles wouldn't beat her when she was so close to giving birth. Surely, this would be their "peace child."

I imagine that at this point in Claire's story it's tempting for the reader to think that Charles is some kind of psychopathic crazy man. Even as a professional, I had to remind myself that this portrait of the batterer was very common. Some 28 million American women have husbands or boyfriends like Charles. Charles is not unique.

I asked Claire, "When he's not this monster you portray, what does he do or say or enjoy?"

"Not much," she replied. "At school, of course, he's a charmer. Good sense of humor. He has a circle of friends and acquaintances and professional associates who think he, and we, are just wonderful. Through the years I have attended all the school functions and have worked at building for him a social façade that makes it appear that he has a super home and family. But he doesn't work at home. His school business is all done at the office, and when he gets home—well, he has no hobbies. He doesn't watch much TV, go out much, listen to music much, or do much of anything. He just exists, gets mad, and beats me."

In short, Charles was a smoothie around town, known and respected and even liked; at home he was a bitter pill and a nobody.

Well—he wasn't always a bitter pill. Occasionally, he showed Claire a good time, taking her out to a movie and then to an expensive restaurant. Claire was aware they couldn't afford it—or that *he* couldn't afford it, and eventually the expense would wind up charged to her checking account. Still, these rare times together showed Claire flashes of the man she thought she had married. Charles could, after all, be tender and considerate. This made it even harder for Claire to react to Charles's transgressions. Whenever she'd consider leaving him, he'd become charming and loving.

One Friday night was just such an evening. They had great fun. They both dressed to the hilt for the occasion, and walking into the movie in full formal evening dress, they felt like teenagers again, playing a role.

Later, at a restaurant called King Arthur's Court, they enjoyed a sumptuous meal and, for once, warm and stimulating conversation. As Charles talked about his dreams, his future, his face was filled with enthusiasm, and the smile he flashed from time to time was contagious. Claire found herself smiling a lot, and as she watched Charles she could feel her love for this man rise up in her anew. Gone were the thoughts of violence and fear and abuse. Here, in this place, this temporary Camelot, time seemed to stop, the past could be forgotten, and a sort of chivalry began to flourish.

Perhaps there is hope, Claire thought.

But the magic of King Arthur's Court would always evaporate into thin air by the time the weekend was out. It seemed Charles held the magician's wand. He was the one who could create such enchanted kingdoms. And he could also very quickly bring them toppling to the ground.

Claire came to compare these romantic interludes to cotton candy. Sweet—but nothing's there. She relished these times for the respite they provided from the abuse, but she knew they weren't real and wouldn't last. Eventually, the tension would build within Charles once again. They'd be reminded that their abode was not a castle but a split-level. And then Charles, looking more like the evil Mordred than the handsome Lancelot, would go on a tear one more time.

Often financial problems seemed to be what set Charles off. In those early years, school teachers weren't making much money. Yet Charles had a craving for the good life. He bought a new car that required just short of half his monthly income for the payment.

"That's the way it's always been," Claire said. "All I've ever heard from him is, 'I don't have anything. Everybody has this and everybody has that, and I'm getting older, and the things I planned to have I'm just not getting.'"

For years, Claire bought that line. Not wanting him to get all worked up, she was eager to do anything to keep him content, or at least calm. She bought him everything he wanted, every gadget he could think of, every trinket he craved. There were snowmobiles and motorcycles and cars and rings and stereos and Tv sets and watches and games and sports equipment—anything Charles wanted, he got. But the craving hole was deep and had no bottom. He made lists. Sometimes he would say, "This is my final list. When I have these things, I will have all I want." But before Claire could get halfway through the list, items would be added.

Claire eventually realized that Charles would never be satisfied. Still, the happier she was able to make him, the less she would be abused. Furthermore, it was Claire's nature, because of her upbringing, to be responsible with money. Bills were paid to the penny. She saw that if she needed something for herself or the house, she'd have to get it herself. But if she was ever short of cash and asked Charles for five dollars, he'd remind her later that she owed it to him. There were separate checking accounts. His and hers. Only hers was for him too.

As I listened to Claire, I developed a feeling of pity for Charles. I saw in this man a deep insecurity. His greed was borne out of his sense of personal incompetence. He grappled desperately with life, trying to make himself worth something. Only he was doing it the wrong way. In the process, he was tearing himself apart. And destroying Claire.

A thought struck me. Charles's obsessive jealousy, so evident during courtship, seemed to have disappeared during the marriage. Jealousy was also a sign of insecurity, a deeper, more personal insecurity. I would have expected to have heard more about it from Claire. It seemed to have gone. Or had it?

"There's so much to say," Claire replied. "I've forgotten about that. I guess I've gotten so used to it. But it hadn't died;

it was as much a part of Charles as it ever was. Whenever I would go with him to a school function, some social gathering, or a party, I usually was pretty quiet. Charles was Mr. Personality, and they were *his* people, not mine. Inevitably, though, I would talk with people. They'd come up to me and we'd chat. Charles would find a reason why we'd have to leave early. In the car he'd let me have it. He'd want to know why a particular guy was so interested or friendly—whatever. He demanded from me whether I was seeing this guy or sleeping with that guy. I denied it every time."

"Because it was untrue?" I asked.

"Of course."

"Were you ever unfaithful to your husband during your marriage?"

"I had the chance more than once. More than a few times, I should say."

"But were you ever unfaithful?"

> Little girl, I say to you, arise.
> *Jesus, to Jairus' daughter*
> *(Mark 5:41, RSV)*

Five
The Permanent Covenant

"No."

It got to the point where Claire refused to go with Charles to any such functions because the outcome was so predictable. "I knew what it would be like in the car later on, and I didn't want any part of it. Not only were his accusations untrue, but I did everything I could not to talk with any men. I didn't smile, I didn't encourage conversation, and I looked stiff and awkward. Still he would accuse."

Mike was born in December 1961. He was big, healthy, and happy.

Having the baby bought Claire a little time without abuse. Charles was proud and excited about his firstborn, and Claire's time in the hospital and in bed at home made her less of a target. Financial problems again crept in to spoil it, however. The craving hole could not be filled. Charles expected more and more. Claire eventually had to go to work and leave her baby with a full time sitter.

When Claire had told me that the beatings had lessened in frequency, I assumed she meant that Charles left her alone during several months at the end of her pregnancy, then had only a flare-up or two per month in the years following. She quickly set me straight on that. To her, and rightly so, "less frequent" beatings meant just once a week, rather than two or three. Mike was not the "peace child" that Claire had counted on.

The irony, if being beaten by your own loving husband isn't ironic enough, was that Claire was living, working, and dying for Charles. She lived in fear of his rage. In those days after the birth of Mike, she worked hard, selling home products or cosmetics to help make ends meet and to help Charles acquire all the things he wanted. At the same time she was suffering at his hand.

It wasn't long before a second child, Debbie, was born. If Claire thought that by having another child, she'd once again find a temporary refuge from Charles's wrath, she soon found something different. Claire was beaten badly several times. It was as if Charles couldn't stand the idea of her being out of work for even the few months it would take to have the child and get back on her feet. And, another baby would be more competition. Claire found it difficult to hide her bruises from her physician. At first, she made excuses. Then she quit trying. He knew. She knew he knew. And not much was said.

The physician, however, was worried about Claire and Debbie, because Claire actually lost weight during the pregnancy. The baby was born normal and healthy, thankfully, but as soon as the child could understand what was going on, she took the brunt of Charles's teasing and humiliation. For some reason, he delighted in teasing her until she was in tears. Mike, three years old when Debbie was born, had never once slept through the night. "He was the most nervous child my pediatrician had ever seen," Claire reported. "He was so uptight because of the yelling and fighting in the house that he developed stomach cramps. He had seen my bruises and was affected by it. Who knows what that does to a child?"

As soon as she could, Claire went back to work—this time in an insurance office as a typist and receptionist. At each place Claire worked, Charles was known to all, respected and admired. They looked forward to his dropping in from time to time. They didn't know he was just checking up on Claire to see who had eyes for her. At every one of Claire's jobs it seemed that Charles decided someone was after her, and he badgered her about it until she quit and moved on.

Claire virtually gave up the care of the children those early years, and all the while she had to handle the balancing of the checkbooks where she could see clearly that more than half his money every month went to checks written for "cash." He was left with barely enough in his account for basic household bills. She paid the rest and bought his luxuries.

Shortly after Debbie was born, Claire became the breadwinner for a few months. A teacher strike kept Charles out of work, and he was miserable. During this time, Claire began to think more about a career. She noticed that the people who worked fewer hours and who seemed to have more fun at it made a lot more money than she did. The salespeople in the office, while they worked hard and worked smart, enjoyed themselves; in most cases, they were their own bosses. Claire worked out a career plan for her life: she'd get some schooling, work her way up in the company, and become an insurance rep. It would take time, but it would win her some independence.

Meanwhile, when Charles got back on the job, he maneuvered into a position where he'd never again be put out of work by a strike. He didn't want to be hurt again with no work, and, ironically, he became the budget director for the school board. Surprisingly, he did a great job, was sent to conferences and seminars, and even earned honors in his work. Still, at home the finances were a shambles.

"I let him try to handle the checking account for a couple of months," Claire said, "but all he did was pay five dollars on each bill and put the rest in his account. I had to take it back to keep us from going bankrupt."

Claire stopped riding in the car with Charles. There were so many arguments and shouting matches that she couldn't take it any more. And worst of all, for as quiet as she had been about the abuse he had dished out—in fact no other person anywhere had a full idea of what was going on—Charles began confiding in his secretary that his wife worked too much, made him work around the house too much, left him with the kids too often, and neglected the family.

Charles's special confidences backfired. Claire explained: "His secretary was the best friend of my cousin. My cousin got the whole story, told her mother (my aunt), who told my mother. My mother told my sister, and my sister came to see me. It went through five people and it remained intact. What came out of my sister's mouth in the form of questions was the same thing I had been hearing from Charles for years. Before beating me, he would berate me for working too much and neglecting the family. But if I worked less and brought home less money, I got hassled for *that*. I couldn't win. And now my sister was saying the same things to me."

"It's a wonder you didn't start to believe it yourself," I said.

"No chance. I told my sister the truth."

"You did?"

"Most of it."

"How much?"

"Enough so that at least my mother and dad would know my side of the story and not assume that I was a bad wife."

"It was still important to you then that you be viewed as a good wife and mother?"

"Of course. Especially for my parents to know that. They had raised me with that in mind. They had instilled in me this idea that I had entered into a covenant that was not to be broken. The only way out of it was adultery on the part of the other person, and even then you were not free to remarry. So there I was, barely twenty-one, the mother of two, with the option of being in a bad marriage or being single the rest of my life. I wanted my children to have a father. I kept thinking things had to get better."

"You thought that kind of marriage was better than being single?"

"Apparently I did."

"How did your sister react?"

Claire thought for a moment. "Just like most people react. She really didn't believe me. I suppose if I had been barely breathing, or if I had been bleeding from my mouth, she would have." Claire paused a moment, looking blankly at the wall. "*You* even find it hard to believe me, don't you, Esther?"

"Yes." I said. "But I *do*."

Claire looked at me and then broke down. It was a small moment of healing. Someone had finally believed her.

In a late 1970s study of battered women, Lenore E. Walker, author of *The Battered Woman,* found certain personality characteristics common among women who have been abused:

1. Has low self-esteem.
2. Believes all the myths about battering relationships.
3. Is a traditionalist about the home, strongly believes in family unity and the prescribed feminine sex-role stereotype.
4. Accepts responsibility for the batterer's actions.
5. Suffers from guilt, yet denies the terror and anger she feels.
6. Presents a passive face to the world but has the strength to manipulate her environment enough to prevent further violence and being killed.
7. Has severe stress reactions, with psychophysiological complaints.
8. Uses sex as a way to establish intimacy.
9. Believes that no one will be able to help her resolve her predicament except herself.

Not all of these characteristics were evident in Claire—or at least not yet. But some were very apparent.

Of these, numbers three and nine were the most interesting to me. Claire was obviously a traditionalist with strong religious convictions about the home, family, and marriage. Furthermore, Claire had been plagued, until now, by characteristic number nine: she felt she was the only one who could resolve the problem.

Time and time again, she told me she had felt trapped. There was no place to go, no place to hide. This was why she had stayed with Charles so long—she didn't believe there were any other options. She had to handle it herself.

Through Claire's sister, word did get back to Claire's parents. It wasn't the whole story, but it was enough for Claire's mother and father to want her out of that home and out from under Charles's abuse. But Claire stayed. She wanted a better life, and she wanted it within the marriage.

Charles was not insensitive to the problem. Little things he said from time to time gave Claire hope. He looked forward to small pleasures like getting away for a few days and visiting his parents, always adding that "things will be better." He seemed to know that Claire was miserable and that he was making her that way.

But those other times, when he would threaten Claire or the children, Claire would wonder why she stayed. Sometimes Charles would threaten to get rid of them all if Claire ever told anyone or tried to get back at him. She said she didn't want to get back at him—just to be safe and get him some help. At this, Charles would be offended.

So the move into town, the two children, the new job, the extra money did little good. A few people knew there was trouble in the marriage, but no one knew enough to be deeply concerned. So nothing changed. Charles had a better job now; he was moving up, an administrator in one of the bigger schools in the district, active in civic affairs, and highly regarded socially. The beatings continued.

If anything wore on Claire's health other than the physical abuse, it was the profane language. The constant swearing was foreign to Claire. She never got used to it. "It grated on me," Claire said, "especially when he took the Lord's name in vain, which was many dozens of times a day. He could hardly speak a sentence without that or some other gutter words."

Two things gave Claire a better perspective on the sickness of her situation with Charles: her career and her children. As she became more and more successful, Claire was able to talk with other salespeople on their own level, rather than as a subordinate. Her job began to require more decision-making —and Claire found she was good at it. Slowly, she developed a respect for herself she hadn't had before. She found out she was good at something; she was worthwhile as a human being. She began to see that Charles had no right to treat her the way he did.

The other eye-opener for Claire was the way Charles treated their daughter Debbie.

Claire: All this time he was abusing Debbie by teasing her until she'd cry and cry. It wasn't the normal fatherly teasing that will make a child laugh and have fun. This was cruel. If he had ever laid a hand on her, I would have killed him.
Mrs. Olson: Do you realize what you just said?
Claire: Absolutely.

Mrs. Olson: I want to know why you feel that Charles would deserve to be killed if he hurt your children, but not when he abused you.

Claire: I don't know. I've never thought about it.

Mrs. Olson: Never thought about killing him?

Claire: Oh, I've wished him dead. There was a time when I *would* have killed him with a knife if he had come closer.

Mrs. Olson: Did that happen here, at this time?

Claire: No. Later.

Mrs. Olson: Let's save it. I want to get this chronologically, because the sequence of what you thought and felt is important. We need to know precisely when it is that you feel you've had enough.

Claire: Don't you think I took enough punishment?

Mrs. Olson: What's important is what you think, Claire.

Claire: (Angrily.) Stop playing psychiatrist with me. What do you think?

Mrs. Olson: Of course you took enough punishment. You took way too much. Ten times too much. A hundred times too much. The fact you press me on this indicates you're not sure.... Oh, Claire.... What I'm looking for is this: What in the world does it take to push you to your breaking point?

Claire: You mean like when I first threatened divorce?

Mrs. Olson: Yes, tell me about that.

Claire: (After a pause.) Esther, do you believe in divorce?

> I am the resurrection
> and the life.
> *Jesus, to Martha the sister
> of Mary
> (John 11:25, RSV)*

Six
The "Good" Years

Claire's question tugged us into another dimension of the client-counselor relationship. The spiritual dimension.

Both Claire and I were born-again Christians; that is, we each had a personal relationship with Jesus Christ. (Our common faith was one of the reasons Claire came to visit me in the first place.) So far, we hadn't talked much about Christianity. But we both felt it—Christ was present when we met together. It reminded me of the verse in Matthew: "For where two or three are gathered together in my name, there am I in the midst of them." I knew a time would come soon when our faith would play a more prominent role in our sessions.

This did not mean that Claire's situation would be resolved by wholly spiritual answers. Healing would not take place merely by her going to church or reading the Bible. But I felt that God often worked through established psychological processes and therapies. And I felt that our common faith in Jesus Christ was good ground on which to develop a therapy program.

I felt strongly that a counselor's authority should not overlap into moral and religious areas: I had no business telling Claire what to believe or what was right and wrong. At the same time, it was my conviction that spirituality and psychology were intimately connected. I knew that Jesus Christ was very important to Claire, just as he was to me, and I suspected that Claire was hurting as much in her spirit as in her psyche.

In fact I wondered if the abuse Claire suffered at the hand of her husband had damaged her image of God. Christian women find themselves in a religion permeated by masculine imagery: the way a woman relates to God the Father and God the Son derives somewhat from the way she relates to the men in her life—her father and her husband. Claire's father was a strong, tender, compassionate man; her husband was the opposite: weak, rationalizing, and abusive. How did this affect Claire's daily walk with God?

There were other questions too, mostly moral or doctrinal problems that only a Christian would face. How did Claire feel about the Apostle Paul's call for wives to submit themselves to their husbands? What about Christ's command to "turn the other cheek"? Did Claire have a responsibility to help her husband find Christ? What did her marriage vows—"for better or for worse"—mean to her? How did Claire incorporate the New Testament theme of forgiveness into her life?

There was no doubt in my mind that for a Christian wife the problem of abuse presented a double whammy. Not only did the abuse threaten Claire physically and psychologically, it cornered her spiritually as well.

I began to realize how long and bumpy a road Claire and I had ahead of us. As a counselor, I would need God's help. From now on, both Claire and I, each for different reasons, would be more aware of the fact that Christ was sitting in on our sessions.

"Esther, do you believe in divorce?" she was asking me. She leaned forward in the easy chair, her hands clenched tightly around a handkerchief. That white handkerchief with the pink embroidery had become familiar in our sessions together. Claire had cried a lot the first few visits. Less often more recently. But her hands were still tense, and her body still displayed that peculiar rigidity.

"It's not my job as a counselor to tell you about Christian doctrine," I said. "The issue of divorce is something for you to decide."

"Well, I know what the Bible says," Claire replied. "I just want to know what *you* say."

"That's even worse. It's not right for my authority to supplant biblical authority."

"It won't. I'm not asking you what's right and wrong. I'm not asking you the *counselor*. I'm asking you the *woman*."

Claire wanted to know what another person would do in her place. She was groping for what was expected of her as a woman. "All right," I said. "I'll take off my counselor's cap. I'll tell you what I think. As another woman. Just remember, it's only my opinion. It's not necessarily any better than your opinion."

"Got it."

I gave myself a moment to collect my thoughts and then continued. "What I believe in, Claire, is your using whatever device is necessary to protect your life and the lives of your children. That man was crushing you, and regardless of what our theological leanings may be on divorce, no one can tell you that it's God's will to allow yourself to be beaten to death at the hands of your husband. Life is sacred—the Bible teaches that, too. Separate, run away, hide, anything. Say anything, do anything, threaten anything to avoid being killed. At some point that might mean divorce. Satan is the author of death. God isn't. No one will fault you for protecting your own life."

"Even to the point of lying?" Claire asked.

"Of course. If a murderer came into your home and demanded to know where your child was, would you tell him the truth?"

"I probably would have, years ago."

"What are you saying?"

"I was taught to tell the truth. God would take care of the consequences."

"But *we* have a responsibility for the consequences too."

Claire looked at the floor. Her finger drew something imaginary on the arm of the chair. "When I promised Charles that I wouldn't tell on him, I meant it. I kept my promises."

"That's the reason you never told anyone except a little bit to your parents and your sister?"

Claire nodded and her eyes met mine again. "I'm glad to

hear what you said about lying to protect your life. I broke—that is, I couldn't keep that promise the last time."

"I want to hear about that."

"OK," Claire said. I thought I detected a faint smile on her face—at least as much of one as I had ever seen from Claire. "That sounded like your counselor's voice again," she said. "Have you put your counseling cap back on?"

I laughed. "Yes," I said. "I'm a counselor again. But that doesn't mean I stop being a woman."

"Neither do I," Claire replied.

After eight years of marriage, at the age of twenty-five, Claire gave birth to another girl, Tricia. The beatings before and after the pregnancy followed the pattern established before Debbie was born. Charles devised new and clever ways to abuse Claire that were less obvious to doctors. Choking, slapping, and verbal abuse usually didn't leave permanent marks. But once again, miraculously, the child was born healthy.

Tricia's birth led Claire to think more deeply about the effect Charles was having on the children. He never abused them physically, although he continued to tease Debbie unmercifully. With Mike he had developed some semblance of a father-son relationship.

But Claire had noticed a kind of antagonism in Mike toward his father, a dislike that couldn't be explained by the normal stages of child growth. Mike had just turned eight, and more and more expressive of his dissatisfaction with the way things were. Of course, Charles often acted like a little boy himself from time to time, and Claire noticed that these were the occasions when Mike seemed to dislike his father most.

Debbie was the opposite. She tended to withdraw from the family, to find a corner of the house away from her mommy and daddy where she could play. She was six and in first grade. She learned to read fast, fascinated by the worlds it opened to her, and as her reading ability developed, she escaped more and more into stories and books. However, it was possible that this was the normal pattern for a middle child. It wouldn't be clear until later precisely what effect

Claire and Charles's constant yelling and fighting would have upon the children. And so far, Claire believed the children hadn't seen any of the physical abuse firsthand. Charles was careful about that.

Soon after Tricia was born, Claire returned to work at the insurance company, at first part time, then later resuming a full schedule. Oddly enough, the job didn't seem to bother Charles too much, although he still put Claire in a bind by complaining that she wasn't home enough. It was true she couldn't win—if she stayed home, Charles would complain they needed more money; when she worked, Charles complained she was neglecting the children—it was the old story. However, when Claire was working it seemed things were better. Charles liked having the extra money, and he also secretly liked the idea that they could afford to hire a babysitter every day—to his thinking, it was something like having a servant or a maid, and it made him feel more affluent.

But the beatings continued.

What Charles did not perceive was that Claire, by working at a career, was becoming less and less dependent. Even if she didn't have freedom in a physical, tangible sense, she became more and more free-thinking, and visions of what life might be like without Charles started to dance in her head.

It quickly brought Claire to the day when she threatened divorce.

"Did you mean it," I asked, "or was it just leverage?"

"Well, it was more than just leverage. I knew it would scare Charles to death. I had learned that he clung to me, needed me—I know it sounds strange—I was his security and his image and everything." Claire adjusted herself in her chair, crossed her legs, and caught her breath. "You know, even now I feel terrible. *Divorce.*"

"You were doing what you had to do."

"I guess. But I'll always wonder if there was something more I could have done... something different—" Claire began to cry.

"But you're still with him."

"But I used divorce as a threat—"

"In self-defense."

"I guess." Claire's eyes were red. A tear rolled down her cheek.

"Claire," I said firmly, "What Charles did to you was not your fault."

"I know that."

"You know, and you don't know. Part of you knows. Another part of you blames yourself."

"Maybe you're right," she said.

After a break, Claire continued. "We had lived in town then for eight years, maybe nine. It had been a long time since I had first threatened to leave Charles if we didn't move closer to some neighbors. I hadn't given many ultimatums since then. I knew the threat of divorce would keep Charles behaved for a few weeks, but I was more serious about it than that."

"So when you made the threat, you fully intended to carry it out."

"Fully. I talked to the girl in our office who had had the insurance company's lawyer handle her divorce. She was satisfied with how he had handled it and with the price, so I started thinking seriously about making an appointment with him. I didn't tell Charles."

"You didn't?"

"No."

"Then you *were* serious."

"Right."

"And you were thinking for yourself."

"Besides that, I told my sister more about what was going on. She and her husband were outraged. They wouldn't share all of it with my parents, but they were upset enough to sit me down and tell me that no one was expected to live that way, Christian or not."

"Right."

"That next day I'd decided I'd had enough."

It was a Friday night and Claire was working late. Charles had called three times that day to make sure she was there. This wasn't uncommon; in some ways, it was this constant surveillance that bothered Claire the most. Once Charles called and didn't even ask to talk with her; he just asked the receptionist if Claire were there, and then he hung up.

That drove Claire past the limit. The lawyer's office was nearby and still open. Claire told the lawyer everything. This was the first person outside of the family that Claire had told. (There were, of course, doctors who had deduced what was happening, but Claire had never discussed it with them.)

Claire's lawyer said that papers would be served the following Tuesday, forcing Charles to move out of the house. This would hold unless Claire contacted the lawyer to do differently.

While Claire was gone, Charles called the office again. He left an urgent message for her to call back.

She did. Charles demanded to know where she had been. She told him.

"I've been to a lawyer," she said, surprising herself with her calmness. "It's over."

"What?" Charles was furious. Claire could imagine him at home, his face becoming red with rage, and his muscles tensing.

"That's right."

"You can't do that."

"Yes, I can. I should have done it long ago."

"Claire . . . uh, shouldn't you think about it some more? You're not thinking clearly."

As Charles's initial rage melted into desperation, Claire felt the first tremors of fear in her voice. "I know what I'm doing."

"Say, you know, I was thinking today—uh, it's about time we found ourselves a new place to live. We've lived here for—what?—seven years—"

"Nine."

"Right. Nine years. It's time for us to move, honey."

"It won't work, Charles," Claire said. "Don't push this."

"Hey. You know me. I've been trying to work out this problem . . . I've said before that I'm sorry for those . . . you know, it won't happen ever again. I promise."

Claire waited in silence on the other end of the line.

"There's a house for sale on the other side of town. I saw it in the paper. Good price. It's bigger. Sounds like the kitchen's huge. We could drive over there tomorrow and look it over—"

"I don't want to live out in the country again," Claire said.

"Oh, no, you won't have to. This is a development house—"

Claire interrupted him again. "Charles," she said, "the papers will be served on Tuesday."

"This isn't fair, honey. Why don't you come home and we'll talk about it? Don't do anything rash. I promise, Claire, you'll be talking to a new guy. I don't know why I've been this way, and I know I've promised to change before, but this time will be different. This time it's for real. And if I ever try anything again, I won't even try to stop you from divorcing me. I just need another chance. You've got to be patient with me. We'll start over."

Claire felt free. She had done it. She was able to hang up, clean up her desk, go home, and face him. She felt she had gained the upper hand.

When she got home, she was greeted by his tears. He made all kinds of promises. He said he thought she ought to have a new car. He knew they needed some new furniture. It would be hers, he said. And he'd be a new person.

Somehow, somewhere between the time she went home that night and the end of the weekend, Claire decided Charles was worth one more try. She called off the dogs.

Mrs. Olson: I see a pattern here in Charles. I've wondered if you've noticed it too.
Claire: What's that?
Mrs. Olson: His approach to handling problems: start all over, move, buy something, change the environment.
Claire: Yes, that's right. He'd always promise to buy me something; it was as if he thought a new house or car or whatever would make everything all better.
Mrs. Olson: It was easier for him to change the environment than to change himself.
Claire: Maybe. But he tried. I believe he tried.
Mrs. Olson: Are you sticking up for him now?
Claire: I don't know, am I? Sometimes I don't know what I'm doing. And here, am I crying again?
Mrs. Olson: Tears are healthy. Take your time. Collect your

thoughts. (A pause.) I'm curious about that: were you just then sticking up for Charles?

Claire: (After a minute of thought.) I think I feel sorry for him. But, no. I'm not sticking up for him. Those are the facts. He did *try*. For a time, things *were* better. . . .

The beatings stopped. They bought a new house. Claire quit her job.

Charles kept his hands off Claire. His restraint was considerable, because he still got angry from time to time. There was less tension in the home. The kids were happier. It was an especially good development for young Tricia. It looked as if she might be able to grow up in a tranquil home.

The house they bought was not the house Charles had talked about that night. It was newer and roomier. It wasn't out in the country, but it was out of town and more secluded. Claire didn't mind: the house seemed to make Charles happy. He had changed.

Claire was exhausted—more than she realized. The doctor put her into the hospital for a few weeks and she cried for days. Maybe it was relief. Maybe depression.

In any case, after Claire grew stronger, she went to school, enrolling in a program that would give her a B.A. and a concentration in business. Charles's reaction to this was *a*typical. He was proud of her, talked about her accomplishments to his friends, and tried to make things easier for her around the house. Money was as tight as ever, but a lot seemed to have changed. Claire could hardly believe it.

Still, it wasn't as if Claire had started loving him again. She still found that very difficult. But she was able to bask in the freedom from fear.

After a few years she was able to relax. She wasn't happy, but she was relieved, which was almost as good. Charles kept only two of the promises he had made—refraining from abuse, and a new house. He still didn't go to church, and money remained a bad subject. But he was good with the kids.

"You had a truce," I said. "A cease-fire."

Claire looked over at me. "I guess. We never smiled at each other."

"Do you know that Charles's attitude toward your schooling was highly unusual?"

"No, why?"

I told Claire that in most wife abuse cases, the wife's efforts to improve herself in a career and particularly to advance her education are perceived as a threat. It often is the cause of violence. That Charles was so encouraging didn't fit the pattern. "It could very well have gone the other way," I said.

Claire replied quickly. "He probably felt that it would net him more money in the long run."

"Is it possible that he really cared about you? That he really wanted you to get the degree?"

"I don't know." Claire had suddenly turned negative and bitter.

"You're being uncooperative today," I said. "You seem angry. And you're not talking as freely. Why?"

"I don't know," Claire replied, and then she paused, looking down at the floor, then over to the window, finally gazing on the large painting hung on the east wall of my office. "He wanted me to go to school because it made me dependent on him. He likes to keep me under his thumb."

"OK, let's change the subject. What was your spiritual life like during all these years?"

"During the bad years—I can't remember very well. During the bad years I just barely hung on to what I believed. Or what I thought I believed. I kept going to church, alone, maybe taking the kids to Sunday school. My devotional life was a disaster. My prayer life wasn't good. I always called out to God during the scenes, but it was so desperate. There never was any peaceful quiet time with him. It wasn't the kind of spiritual relationship with God I should have had. What I longed for was a spiritual husband to take the lead in the home, but I can't blame that on him—he wasn't even a Christian. I guess I had a responsibility to stay in tune with the Lord. I didn't do it."

"What you really wanted was a husband you could submit to in a spiritual way?"

"I suppose."

"Did you give the Lord the credit during the good years?" I asked.

Claire replied quickly and angrily. "They weren't all that good." She paused, choking back a sob, trying to control her emotions. "Sorry." She paused again and took a deep breath. "I guess that during those years when he didn't beat me, I kind of chalked it up to God answering my prayers. But I wanted more than just a husband who didn't beat me. I wanted more—I don't know. I was selfish, I think. I wasn't satisfied."

"It's not selfish to want a happy home," I said softly.

"It's not, is it?" Claire replied as if she had needed me to confirm it for her. It was still a question in her mind. "But it's what I thought at the time."

I probed more deeply. "Why does it bother you for me to talk about those years as 'good' years?"

"Because they weren't. Not really."

"Are you afraid our emphasis on these so-called 'good' years might divert attention from the abuse?"

Claire nodded, and I could see she was close to tears. "I'm the one who's suffered. Not him. People might not understand that."

"They do," I said. "*I* do." I moved my chair beside hers. She shook with great, uncontrollable sobs. I put my arm around her and held her as she cried. "Claire," I said. "Look at me. I'm your friend."

> Let her alone, why must
> you make her feel
> uncomfortable?
> *Jesus, speaking to his disciples
> about Mary, the woman who
> anointed his feet with
> costly oil.*
> *(Mark 14:6, Phillips)*

Seven
Saturday Scenes

Charles bought and sold cars as often as new models hit the market. It was a prime cause of disturbance in his life: either the car he had wasn't quite the car he wanted, or the car he had didn't work right. Something was always breaking down —a water pump, an alternator, a switch—and it made Charles mad. The pattern was always the same. When the car would break down, Charles would go to work on it, despite the fact that he really didn't know that much about cars. He'd look into the carburetor and take a screwdriver to it, throwing the timing out of whack. Usually the problem had nothing to do with what Charles was attempting to fix—but he didn't know any better.

It happened on a Saturday. There really wasn't much to it —at least not in physical terms. Some shoving, yelling, and of course Charles's cursing. But it was as if a dark cloud that had once threatened Claire's being had drifted clear around the world and now, from the other side, was entering her life once again. It was over in a minute, like a summer storm, and Charles quickly apologized, but deep down Claire had a sinking feeling that was not to go away.

It happened again three weeks later. Claire heard Charles slam the car door. She listened as the hood went up and Charles tinkered with the engine. Minutes later the hood slammed shut. Charles stomped onto the front porch. There was cursing and yelling. Claire ran to the front door and locked it just as Charles's hand reached the knob. Suddenly his fist crashed through the door panel, splintering the wood. It seemed to shock him as much as it shocked Claire. They stood there on opposite sides of the door, Claire's heart beating fast, Charles breathing hard. But for that the two were silent and seemed to wait in the awkward grip of time for some indication of what to do next.

Charles was quick to beg forgiveness. He pleaded with Claire that she not make any hasty decisions based on this particular incident. After all, he hadn't touched her. And he had the door replaced that afternoon.

Claire was eager to forgive, to return to the days of tranquility, though a part of her knew that they were lost forever. She fell back into the same trap, thinking that if she could help him financially—if he could have the things he wanted—he'd be placated.

There was another reason Claire forgave Charles so easily. She had become aware of the effects a broken home would have upon the kids. Mike was now twelve, a seventh-grader and he was entering difficult years. More and more he was out on his own; he didn't like family gatherings, preferring to be off somewhere with his friends. Debbie was in fourth grade. She had been a model child, although she still seemed a bit aloof and quiet. Tricia was the innocent, a bright and vivacious five-year-old, mostly unaffected by the problems of her parents. Claire realized that a divorce would have devastating effects on her children. What was once an effective weapon to keep Charles at bay had faded into a useless, impractical, empty threat.

By now, Claire had finished school and had rejoined the insurance company where she had worked before. Her business education qualified her as a field representative for the firm, and she was assigned locally. Later she'd travel more widely. Still, she was more on her own, making money, making decisions, making business friends. She was running with a classier crowd, and she loved it. Charles complained that she wasn't home enough. But in fact, she was home more now than when she had been attending school.

Charles had been promoted to assistant principal. Their

income and community stature were higher than ever. Even so, Charles always seemed to want more than they could afford. They always lived beyond their means, whatever their means were.

The abuse, which had abated for several years, now continued and worsened. Claire could detect a pattern, a cycle of various attitudes or behaviors that seemed to characterize the abuse. First, the tension would build up in him until it seemed he would explode. During this stage every little thing seemed to annoy him: finances, the car, the way Claire talked to him, his work, his schedule, going out evenings with people he didn't want to be with, etc. Then, the second phase of the cycle would be the violence, the beatings. In other words, he *would* explode; it was as if he were a time bomb—after a while Claire was able to predict when Charles would go off. Finally, after the incident of abuse, there would come the part of the cycle that seemed so strange and by now had become so recognizable—Charles's contrite, loving behavior. (Claire didn't realize it when she described this cycle of abuse to me, but her observations are verified by many sociologists. In fact, there is a cycle "theory" which asserts that these same three stages—build-up, explosion, and remorse—are universal and highly predictable.)

The abuse seemed often to occur on Saturdays. It got to the point where Mike would get up early Saturday morning and watch television until he heard his father stirring; then he would leave and be gone the rest of the day. He knew a fight would start. None of the children brought their friends home anymore, because they didn't know what to expect.

Claire still refused to ride in the same car with Charles. When they visited their in-laws, however, they rode together. Charles would drive. When they were going to *his* parents' house, Charles never caused trouble. He would be quiet and cooperative. When they visited *her* parents' place out in the country, however, they wouldn't be in the car more than five minutes before Charles was verbally abusive. He would blow up about any little thing—the weather, the car, the price of gasoline. If Claire dared argue with him, he'd scream at her, pull her hair, and shove her against the door—while he was driving. The car would be all over the road.

As these Saturday scenes became regular, Claire tried a new tactic: silence. Rather than forgive Charles, she would say nothing at all. She'd go to bed and stay there for hours.

Charles couldn't stand it. He'd treat her like a queen, falling all over himself to apologize and help out around the house. He'd speak softly, act humble, and watch his manners and behavior. By Sunday he'd be beside himself, wondering if he'd be forgiven. He was concerned mostly that Claire might tell someone at church. Every chance he got, when the kids weren't present, he'd get up close to Claire and badger her with earnest questions: "Are you sure you're all right? You're not still mad at me are you? You're not going to do anything rash? You wouldn't go to a lawyer or anything? You're not going to tell anyone, are you?"

It was sickening. Still she couldn't bring herself to threaten him aloud. Later Sunday night her silence would turn to sarcasm: "No, for the sake of the kids I'm not going to do anything this time. Your reputation and your job will survive, even though they shouldn't."

Charles's childishness affected every part of his personality, except at work. There he continued to excel and impress. (Hardly a person he has ever worked with in school administration would believe this story about Charles. But of course, they'll never hear it unless he tells it. As is so often the case in abuse situations, people hear about the poor victim, but the perpetrator is protected.) But at home Charles's behavior became more extreme. Whenever Claire's family showed up, Charles would suddenly complain of an upset stomach and disappear to the bedroom for the rest of the evening. He used the same excuse for leaving church and parties and banquets. (But he got sick only during *Claire's* activities.)

Meanwhile Claire didn't know what to do about his compulsive spending. Before, he had made lists of things he wanted. Now he went on mad buying binges. He bought and sold cars two, three, four times a year; and they almost always had three or four in the driveway. But even with all his extravagance, Charles didn't wind up with the things he wanted. He'd find himself, after the dust had cleared, with a small economy car with no air conditioning. At home, it would become a major issue.

Was there anything during this time in Charles's life that might explain these changes in behavior?

Claire: None that I can think of. He just changed.
Mrs. Olson: Were the changes permanent or temporary?
Claire: Temporary. And they weren't big changes. I mean they were subtle. I was the only one who'd noticed.
Mrs. Olson: There wasn't anything—any event—in Charles's life that might have caused him to act differently?
Claire: Believe me, by this time I was looking for anything that might explain his behavior. There were the diet pills—but that was later.
Mrs. Olson: Let's save it, then.
Claire: He was always being promoted at work. But that wasn't anything new. There were education conventions he went to once a year. There was the reunion. There were some times when his mother was ill—but not seriously.
Mrs. Olson: What reunion?
Claire: High school.
Mrs. Olson: He attended his high school reunion?
Claire: In style. He had made a list of the things he wanted for it. It was of course, absurd—a Lincoln Continental, a flashy diamond ring, a new wardrobe. Also he wanted to have a principalship by then.
Mrs. Olson: This wasn't the same school district, was it?
Claire: Oh, no. Another part of the state. Anyway, he bought the new wardrobe. I helped pay for the ring.
Mrs. Olson: Did you go with him?
Claire: Yes. He wanted to show me off.
Mrs. Olson: Ironic.
Claire: I said I'd go with him if he'd go with me to an insurance convention later in the year. I don't know why—I was pleased when he agreed to it.
Mrs. Olson: Bad choice?
Claire: You said it.

For most of the convention, Charles had acted like a perfect gentleman. It lasted only a day and a half, and he was his basic charming public personality. But the occasion gave him many opportunities to worry about who was talking to Claire, what they were saying, why she was enjoying herself so much, and so on.

The last session went a little long. The convention speaker tried to wrap up all the loose ends. Charles was fidgeting and quite ready to go when it ended. He managed cordial goodbyes all around, but by the time he and Claire had pulled out of the parking lot and onto the highway, he was swearing.

He accused Claire of flirting, of ignoring him, of trying to play up to people. He accused her of talking about him behind his back. He complained that the meetings were boring, the rooms hot, the sleeping quarters cramped, the bathrooms not private enough. He griped about the price of gas, the lack of air conditioning in his car, and what the wind did to his hair when he had to drive with the windows open.

Claire did everything she could to placate him. Rather than defend herself or argue, she apologized for doing anything that looked like flirting, saying, "I certainly wouldn't want to embarrass you or make you feel bad that way."

Three hours later he was still fuming, though she hadn't given him anything to fume about. Charles became more agitated. Once, he reached over and grabbed for her throat. She just pulled away and tried to keep him calm. Deep down, she wanted to scream at him, to tell him that she would never, ever ride with him again. But she knew this wasn't the time.

Nothing worked. Within ten miles of home he swerved off the road trying to get at her. He punched her arm and tried to pull her hair. She screamed and wrenched herself away, then tried to slap him as Charles quickly pulled the car back from the shoulder and onto the blacktop once again. He was boiling. By the time they had pulled into the driveway there had been several minutes of shoving and pushing. As Claire got out of the car, Charles seemed to cool off a bit, but Claire felt she couldn't take a chance. While he put the car away, she fished in her purse for her house key, went around to the front door, unlocked it, and pushed it open. But instead of going inside, she continued around the side of the house and ran up the side of a small knoll in the darkness. From there she could clearly see the house and Charles pacing about inside it.

It wasn't long before he discovered she wasn't in the house.

"Claire," he called. "Claire!" There was panic in his voice and the fear of being found out. He walked out onto the back porch and called Claire's name again and again into the deep of night. Outside, he tried to sound nonchalant—obviously much aware of the neighbors, though they were nearly a hundred yards away. He walked around the yard, then back into the woods, and finally to the foot of the knoll behind which Claire sat.

"For some reason I had a delicious, tingly feeling," Claire said, "being able to see everything he was doing and knowing that I was getting to him, scaring him." Claire was more animated now as she told me about this, but then a cloud quickly passed over her face. "That's wrong, isn't it? To want to see him hurt and scared."

"It's not wrong to express to me the way you felt then," I said. "I want to know what was going on inside you at the time."

"But it was wrong to have felt that."

"Maybe. But understandable. It was a reaction to evil."

Claire shifted in her seat, looked out the window, then continued. "The only thing that would have made me feel better about that situation would have been if Charles had known that I could see him, but couldn't do anything about it."

"You wanted power over him."

"Is that what I wanted?" Claire looked straight at me, into my eyes. It occurred to me that since our first session, Claire's disposition had changed considerably. She was still crying frequently, and occasionally she would get stubborn and wouldn't want to talk anymore. But her eyes were more likely to seek out mine in our conversations, and she was able to hold her gaze longer—her eyes no longer such a giveaway of all she'd been through.

"Then I heard him go to the neighbors," Claire said, "and ask them to help him find me. When they split up to look for me, I walked out toward the road where our neighbors were and told them I thought everything would be OK now. I felt I could go home without any hassle."

"And was it safe?"

"Yes. Charles was so remorseful that I almost wanted to

forgive him that night. But I waited until the next morning."

I couldn't help but smile. Claire had finally begun maneuvering, letting Charles take some heat. She wouldn't forgive him right away anymore. She'd wait until it suited her timing. It was a step—an important step—but it wasn't enough.

"It was about that time that I went to a special meeting at church," Claire said, "a women's group meeting, or something like that, and the message that was given that night really affected me. We were told that a woman's relationship with God was *her* responsibility, not her husband's. A woman couldn't count on her husband to lead a spiritual life *for* her. She had to do it herself."

"And did that realization help change the situation at home?" I asked.

"It did and it didn't. It changed *me*. It didn't change Charles one bit. After that meeting I prayed that God would help me rededicate myself to him, and that I would do what he wanted me to do. I guess I was slowly catching on to the idea that Charles wasn't ever going to be the husband I thought I had married."

"Did things ease up at home then?" I asked.

"They got worse. Even though I didn't tell Charles about it, he must have sensed it. Either that or the demons who possessed him knew that I had changed, because things got a lot worse at home."

I asked Claire if she really believed that Charles was demon-possessed.

"Sometimes I thought so, yes."

"Did you ever tell him that?"

"Yes."

"His reaction?"

"As you would imagine."

"Violent?"

"No, just hurt. But of course I never said it during a beating. Even so, I sometimes wondered why he *didn't* get violent."

I thought about this a moment. Claire had probably succeeded in putting Charles in a corner—a dangerous thing to do but perhaps in this case it had worked. Charles couldn't react violently to Claire's suggestion of demon possession because that would've proven Claire right. "Charles may have been more calculating than he let on." I said.

"I came to think so," Claire replied.

"Do you think this was the right thing to say to him—this business of demon possession?"

"Of course not," Claire said quickly, "but I *never* knew the right thing to say. It was rare that I was ever able to say exactly how I felt about what he had done to me."

I saw tears well up in Claire's eyes. She went on: "He's ruined more than half my entire life, made me miserable, ashamed, humiliated, depressed, angry, hurt. How can I tell him that? And when? Only when he's apologizing? When he's doing that, he's telling *me* what he's done to me. Esther, I *never* knew what to say or do—or anything."

For most of our time together, Claire was composed, but at the times when the enormity of everything struck her, when she started to see the whole tragic picture, she'd break into deep sobs. Within limits, this was good for her. For so many years she had failed to see herself as victim—indeed, she had taken part of the blame. Now that she had finally seen herself more objectively, it hit her, and it hit her hard.

Often as a Christian counselor I walk the fine line between biblical doctrine concerning death to self and the psychological need we all have to love ourselves.

The Bible says, "Take no thought for your life..." (Matt. 6:25); "Resist not evil: but whosoever shall smite thee on thy right cheek, turn to him the other also" (Matt. 5:39); "For whosoever will save his life shall lose it: and whosoever will lose his life for my sake shall find it" (Matt. 16:25). In the context of wife abuse, these are chilling verses. The whole of Scripture speaks of self-sacrifice: what is a Christian woman who is abused supposed to think and believe and do?

Psychology says that mental and psychological health is built on a strongly developed self-concept and a sense of self-worth. We counselors speak of *self-actualization* and *ego* and *superego*. Our world is filled with people who feel they are inferior; a person's "worthwhileness" is the major social and psychological problem today. How does a Christian woman who is being abused achieve a proper sense of her own value?

This is the dilemma, and I'm afraid I have no answers. But I do wonder sometimes if there is as much of a dilemma as it might seem. Certainly the Bible teaches the value and the sacredness of human life as well as sacrifice and selflessness. Certainly the point is made in Scripture that each of us is precious in the eyes of our Lord. At the same time, psychologists must recognize that selfishness is as big a problem in our modern world as is the inferiority complex. Charles himself was a good example of a desperately self-seeking human being. (Unfortunately, it is the nature of our society—and of clinical psychology, I might add—to think that Claire was the one who needed help, not Charles.)

This is the place I come to: there must be a difference between a person being self-seeking and self-preserving, between selfishness and positive self-regard, between a preoccupation with self and a healthy integration of self with others in society.

I felt it was consistent with Scripture that Claire develop a strong self-image. The Bible said that God loved her—in fact, that he loved her even before she loved him (1 John 4:19). God keeps watch over the sparrows of the air, and Claire was of even more value (Matt. 10:29, 30). Beyond that, Claire was God's personal creation—he made her. What right, then, did Charles have to destroy that precious creation that God loved so very dearly?

I wanted Claire to come to the point of realizing she was special to God. She was not righteous, of course, not perfect, not even worthy, in a spiritual sense, of God's gifts. But she was special in his sight because he had chosen to love her.

Diet pills were the cause of Charles's problem, or so Claire once thought.

It had been a startling discovery. She had been reading a magazine article about the dangerous effects of diet pills. There were ten symptoms of dexedrine abuse; Charles had eight. It fit him to a T. Claire confronted him with this news when he was in a good mood.

Surprisingly, Charles read the article and agreed with

Claire. And he said he would stop taking the diet pills immediately.

As before, Claire had felt that she had found the root of Charles's problem. Always, there was one important discovery or event that stood between Claire and happiness. Now it was diet pills.

Charles went through a difficult period of withdrawal. He began smoking again, something he had previously given up. He'd never smoke at school and never in the house, so he would sit out on the porch at night and chain smoke two packs of cigarettes. It would take hours. The effect was essentially the same as if he'd taken diet pills. His personality would change, he'd grow restless and angry, he'd become physical and vocal, he'd swear, and ultimately the abusiveness would return. The same old pattern.

So nothing changed. And after a time, Claire realized that the diet pills had had nothing to do with Charles's problem. She remembered that he hadn't always been on diet pills; only for the past several months. The pills couldn't possibly have been the cause of Charles's long history of wife-beating.

As those cool spring nights wore on and as Charles, agitated, puffed away on packs of Dorals, Claire's sudden hope went up in wisps and curls of white smoke.

The next time Claire visited she was smiling. As usual, she was sharply dressed—this time in a natty gray business suit. She was in town to visit an insurance client, and the time conveniently fit into our counseling schedule.

"How are things at home?" I asked as she sat across from me.

"No incidents," she said.

"You mean no *beatings?*"

She nearly laughed, remembering our earlier session when she had corrected me on the same choice of words. "You're right—*beatings.* No beatings. I'm so anxious, I guess, for nothing to happen that I'm afraid of saying the word. Beatings. There, I've said it."

I had to remind myself from time to time as we worked through Claire's case history, that what had happened some years ago—we were up to 1977 now—was not necessarily the case now. She had been living with her husband for some two years now without incident—that is, without a beating. At each session I monitored the situation at home, checking to see if there was any recurrence of the violence. So far, there was nothing.

"Are things *better* at home with Charles?" I asked.

"No, not really. It's stiff. Awkward. But there is no abuse. He's changed."

"But you seem so happy today. Why?"

"I'm beginning to like the idea of getting this out. It's been bottled up inside for so long. It wasn't much fun at first—these sessions—and I suppose *fun* isn't the right word for it even now, but I feel better after our times together. Today, I really looked forward to coming. It hurts, but it helps. You know?"

"I'm glad," I said. "You ready to start right in, or do you want to chat a while?"

"I'm ready. Let's go."

"OK. this could be a rough session."

"I know."

"Let's start with the time Mike got involved. That was after the diet pills thing, wasn't it?"

"Right," Claire replied. "I was late getting home from work."

When Claire drove into the driveway, Charles ran out of the house and berated her before she could even get out of the car. "Where have you been!" he yelled. "Do you know how long I've been waiting?" His face was red, his eyes glazed over with rage.

Claire quickly threw the car into reverse and backed out immediately, but Charles ran after her down the driveway, kicked at the door, and by the force of his kick, fell under the side of the car. Claire braked to avoid hitting him, and Charles grabbed the door handle, pulled himself up, and wrenched open the door—Claire had not had time to lock it.

With one hand in her hair and another under her arm, Charles dragged her into the house. He pushed her into the kitchen and slammed the front door behind him. Claire, falling onto the floor, and against the wall, threw her hands up to cover her face. Her head blasted into the ceramic wall tile. It was the first time in years that Charles had drawn blood. And now it was everywhere.

Charles dropped to his knees, sobbing and pleading for forgiveness. "Please let me take you to get stitches," he said penitently.

"You better believe I'm going to tell them how it happened," Claire said firmly, eyes blazing. But when she got cleaned up, it was discovered that the wound wasn't nearly as serious as it appeared. It was a cut and scrape along the side of the head, but it wasn't deep enough for stitches. Claire elected not to go to the hospital, and Charles took charge and cleaned and dressed the wound.

Mike came home from a date, saw his mother with a bandage around her head, and demanded to know what happened. Claire told him, honestly and frankly. There was no use now in trying to hide it. Mike marched into the bedroom upstairs and confronted his father.

"I didn't—" Charles began.

"I don't want to hear it," Mike hissed. "I know what happened." Claire stepped into the bedroom behind Mike. Charles sat up in the bed cowering against the headboard. Mike leaned close and stuck his face right into his father's. "If you ever touch her again," he said, "I'll kill you!"

Charles turned away and faced the window. "I have an ultiatum too," Claire said firmly. "If you don't get help by August 1, I'm going to divorce you."

> Then Jesus . . . said to her, "Where are your accusers? Didn't even one of them condemn you?" "No sir," she said. And Jesus said, "Neither do I. Go and sin no more."
> *Jesus, to the woman taken in adultery.*
> (John 8:10, 11, TLB)

Eight
Promises, Promises

One of the reasons Claire found it so hard to leave Charles was that he could be so charming and considerate when he was sorry for what he had done. His remorse seemed to be genuine. And when he cried immediately after an incident, he could be so *broken* (even irresistible, much as a child often is after he or she has been punished) that Claire, despite her aches and bruises and the terror of what had gone before, could not bring herself to follow through on her threats to Charles and her promises to herself.

After the most recent ultimatums, the one by Mike and then the threat of divorce from Claire, Charles was like a lamb. Docile, quiet, considerate, charming. Charles treated Claire well, making sure to do little things for her, and showering her with thoughtfulness. Claire wasn't really fooled by him as much as she fooled herself: While she did believe Charles to be truly sorry for his actions, Claire never doubted that his pleasant demeanor was essentially an act. She knew Charles was a master at getting what he wanted, something like that same punished child who, through the tears, rather coldly assesses a parent's vulnerability and is able to transform a bad situation into a new toy. Even so, when Charles acted so charming and compassionate, he reminded Claire of the man she had married, of the dreams she had painfully discarded along the way, and of the hope she had once had of being loved and needed by a husband. At these times Claire allowed herself to be deluded into thinking that the fragments of a shattered marriage could somehow be reassembled and glued back together.

Charles promised Claire a trip to Detroit. It was business for him, but it would offer them "a chance to get away, to eat at some nice restaurants," and to be together. Charles was trying desperately to forestall Claire's threat of divorce.

But he never sought counsel. August 1 came and went. Claire reasoned that she couldn't carry out her threat as long as he was acting so nice. There wasn't just cause, she felt. At the same time Claire berated herself for being cowardly. She badgered herself about this, reminding herself of all the other times she had backed down from carrying out a threat. *Still,* she thought, *it wouldn't be fair to leave him when he is being the perfect husband.*

And this, of course, was precisely what Charles had counted on. But what Charles didn't realize was that he had driven Claire to the wall. He would never know until it was too late that Claire had made a promise to herself—somewhere in that nether region between the conscious and the subconscious—that one more physical incident, no matter how trivial, would spell the end of the marriage.

Through her work, Claire became acquainted with a family that had just moved into the area from Oklahoma. Mr. Stevenson had come to the office inquiring about insurance. Claire soon discovered that he, his wife, and their son were Christians and were now looking for a good local church. Claire recommended her own church to the Stevensons, they had attended, and a relationship was struck up. One Wednesday night, Claire made plans to go out to dinner with them.

Now Charles usually worked late on Wednesday. He found that by working late on Wednesday, he could clear away most of the paperwork before staff meetings on Thursday. And since Charles worked late, Claire arranged her schedule to work late Wednesdays as well. Charles usually had little interest in Claire's church friends; for that matter, he usually had little interest in her interests. So it was not unusual for Claire to consider spending an evening at dinner with some friends from work or church, even though Charles was not present.

This particular Wednesday night, Claire left work at the regular time, and met the Stevensons at the designated restaurant. The Miller's Table was one of the really nice places in the area, and so Mr. and Mrs. Stevenson, their teenage son Randy, and Claire enjoyed a fine dinner and a relaxing conversation.

Afterward, walking back to the cars, Claire sensed something strange. She felt as if she were being watched. She turned, peered into the darkness, and spotted Charles in his car, waiting, watching. Claire said good-bye to the Stevensons and said that she would be in touch with Mr. Stevenson about the insurance policy. "I'll look forward to doing this again sometime," she added. "Bye now."

Claire went to her car and drove to her sister's house, where she knew her parents were visiting.

Charles followed her the whole way, finally pulling up behind Claire in her sister's driveway. "Where the ——— have you been!" he shouted.

Claire saw someone inside pull aside the living room drapes and look out. "Why ask?" Claire replied. "You ought to know. You've been tailing me."

Charles had thought he hadn't been detected. "Who were those people?" he asked finally.

"The Stevensons. From church. If you went more often, you'd know—"

"Who was the guy?" Charles interrupted.

"Their son," Claire replied curtly. "Who did you think?"

Charles didn't answer. Claire knew, however, that he had thought Randy Stevenson to be older; he had thought Claire was on some kind of a double date.

"You know," Claire said, "if I were going to cheat on you, it wouldn't be at The Miller's Table. Charles, you don't make sense! I wouldn't do something like that in public. I wouldn't do it at all, for that matter. But certainly not in public."

Claire knew she'd have to shut up. Charles's rage was building. She could see the blood rush to his face and his muscles tense. He was about to say something, in fact, about to bawl her out, when Claire's sister stepped out the front door and invited them in. All of a sudden, Charles was full of smiles and charm. Charles and Claire stepped inside, and Charles spent the evening overwhelming the family with his humor and good nature.

While he was entertaining the troops, Claire excused herself and called home to see if the kids were there. She didn't know what Charles would be like later. She wouldn't want to be alone.

As it turned out, the evening with the family, from the start an improvisation, lasted long enough to make Charles forget the incident that had gotten him there. Returning home, nothing more was said.

Later, in bed, Claire thought the whole evening had been like a time bomb that fizzled. A scare, a little smoke, but finally a dud. Still, their marriage had suffered a close call. Of that, Claire was very much aware.

(1) A wickedly hot Saturday. (2) A wedding at the church. (3) Dinner with the organist and her husband—Jean and Herb Simpson. (4) No air conditioning in the house. (5) Car trouble. (The car, the car—ever the car....)

Later, Claire would reflect upon that day, make this list, and think that it was simply a combination of ordinary incidents—a conspiracy of circumstances—that brought everything to a boil. It *was* hot that day. *Everyone* was testy, not just Charles. And even *Claire* didn't feel like going to a wedding in that heat.

But Charles *really* didn't want to go to a wedding. It was an imposition upon his Saturday, his time off, his leisure. And he didn't like the Simpsons.

Saturday morning, the sun got up first and made everything sizzling and sweaty by eight A.M. Charles awoke at eight-fifteen. At eight-thirty, Claire awoke to the sound of Charles ranting and raving downstairs. He was swearing about the heat, the humidity, the wedding, and anything else he could think of. The kids straggled downstairs by about nine.

Charles seemed to calm down some after breakfast, and Claire reminded him that the wedding was at three o'clock. "And, remember, dinner with the Simpsons right after the reception," she said.

Charles grimaced but said nothing. Claire and Charles left each other alone until just before they were ready to leave for the church in the afternoon.

Claire realized that sometimes when she talked to Charles about doing something—say, for example, going to the wedding and to dinner that day—she sounded as if she were nagging him. She didn't like to be that way, but she knew if she didn't say *something*, Charles would forget, either accidentally or on purpose. Claire sought ways of reminding him about things that didn't sound like nagging. She still thought sometimes that if she could be a little bit more inventive or creative in the way she spoke to Charles, maybe he wouldn't get so upset. *Maybe he just gets irritated at the sound of my voice,* she thought. *Maybe if I change the way I talk....*

At two-thirty, Claire and Charles left for the wedding—in separate cars, of course. Claire didn't want the hassle of a fight in the car or the inconvenience of Charles getting restless and wanting to take her home early. She pretty well counted on him driving home after the reception and then meeting her and the Simpsons at the restaurant for dinner.

Arriving at the same time, Claire and Charles entered the church and sat in one of the back pews where Herb Simpson was sitting. Jean was at the organ up front. Their pew was actually in an auxiliary seating section behind the main area. Claire was glad for this because it meant that if Charles wanted to leave during the ceremony, he could so do with a minimum of disturbance.

Charles was friendly and jovial with Herb as they sat down, and he made some nice comment about looking forward to dinner later. But when the ceremony started, his attitude changed sharply. Claire soon realized that it had been a mistake for her to sit between Herb and Charles; Charles felt no compulsion to behave. The ceremony had hardly begun when Charles swore out loud about the heat.

Claire cringed. She could hardly believe it. People sitting up ahead turned to stare. Then Charles made a big production of taking off his coat. Herb was more surprised than anything; he still wasn't sure he had heard right: an assumed Christian swearing out loud in church? But there was little doubt about it a bit later when Charles blurted out, "Why the

———— is this preacher taking so much time?"

Herb stared, incredulous. Claire looked down, then away, completely ashamed. Others around them turned and scowled.

When Charles took a breath to say something more, Claire elbowed him hard. "Why don't you just leave if you're going to be this way?" she whispered loudly. Charles ignored her and loosened his tie. Soon the second pastor got up to make some additional comments.

"I can't believe this ————," Charles said as soon as he realized *both* pastors were to speak.

Claire prayed he would be quiet until it was over. Somehow, some way the time did pass; the wedding was over, but not until Charles had grumbled and fidgeted and talked out loud several times more.

Later, Claire noticed that Herb managed to sneak away and put himself toward the front of the reception line. It was clear he had been embarrassed by Charles. Charles was still drawing stares. When he spoke, people recognized him as the one who had uttered the swear words during the wedding.

In the parking lot, Charles was all smiles again. Claire couldn't keep up with his swings of temperament. The Simpsons walked by and said that they would meet Charles and Claire at the restaurant. "We have to stop home first," they said. Herb had a sort of grim look on his face, but Jean was smiling.

"We do too," Claire replied. "Shall we meet you at five?"

Charles sidled up to Herb and said, "Sure was hot in there. Couldn't hardly stand it."

Herb forced a smile. "Yeah. I may even change my shirt at home. I feel like I've just run a marathon."

"It was a little close in there," Jean said. Then, turning to Claire, "Shall we make it five-thirty instead? That would give us just enough time, I would think."

"Fine. See you there."

Walking back to their cars, Claire finally spoke up. "What in the world possessed you to act that way in there?"

He tried to defend himself: the heat, the length of the service, his shirt was too tight around the neck....

"Only a child would act that way. I've had it, Charles."

Claire's eyes were blazing. "I'm not going to take this again. I'm not going to be embarrassed by you anymore."

At home Charles seemed contrite. He was quiet while he changed his shirt. He even seemed to feel a little embarrassed by his behavior. Claire didn't often see this in him, this near submissiveness, this sheepishness. It was practically endearing, and it softened her a little, making her think that maybe the day could be salvaged. "Ride with me in the Mercury," Claire said.

"That's OK," Charles replied quietly.

"Your air conditioning doesn't work. You'll be sweaty before you get there."

"That car never works. Something's always going wrong."

"Ride with me."

"Do you have the money for the meal?" Charles asked.

Claire nodded. That had been the condition, of course: if he had to go out with her and the Simpsons, Claire would have to pick up the tab.

Charles rode with Claire.

Charles seemed calm enough; it was Claire who was tense. She wasn't sure about him, still. She didn't want to shell out fifty bucks on a dinner if he was going to spoil it with a scene. Already, she wasn't sure why the Simpsons had kept the date. Charles's behavior had been so obnoxious; surely Herb was anticipating more of the same. "You'd better behave yourself tonight," Claire said.

Charles swore. "Hold it a sec," he said. "Who are you to tell me how to act?"

"You obviously can't figure it out for yourself."

"Who do you think you are?"

Claire held her own. "I'm sick of your bullying and childishness, Charles. I mean really *sick* of it."

"I don't understand this," Charles said, voice loud and uncontrolled now. "How is it that you get off telling me what to do?"

"If you don't settle down, I'm turning around and going home."

"I didn't want to go to dinner anyway, remember?"

"I'm turning around." Claire made a U-turn in the middle of the highway.

Charles was surprised. And angry. "What the ——— do you think you're doing?"

Claire's eyes filled with tears. She knew what was happening. "I can't go," she said. "I won't go with you like this."

As she turned off the highway into their subdivision, Charles reached over and switched off the ignition key. The power steering died, and Claire fought with all her strength to pull the car over.

Claire was in a long dress and heels—what she had worn to the wedding—but that didn't seem to matter to Charles. He crawled over to her side of the car, climbed on top of her, squeezed her in a bear hug that kept her from breathing, and kicked her hard in the shins.

Somehow, the car had come to a stop at the entrance to their subdivision, and Claire had visions of being beaten by Charles right in front of her neighbors—it was a busy entrance, and everyone went through there. Claire was able to free her hands: with the right she grabbed the keys out of the ignition; with her left she opened the car door.

She could hardly breathe, let alone move, but somehow Claire slithered out from underneath him and tried to run down the road. She threw the keys as far as she could, but she wasn't able to get far in a long gown and heels. Claire screamed at the top of her lungs, but no one heard her. *How many times had that subdivision entrance been filled with traffic? Always, always cars coming and going. Now, not a single car in sight.* Claire's screaming gave Charles the extra shot of adrenaline he needed. He raced down the road, grabbed Claire by her biceps from behind, and dragged her back to the car, throwing her in on the passenger's side. When he pulled out his own set of keys, Claire realized how futile her attempt had been to keep her set from him. She didn't have the strength now to try to escape again. Besides, she was convinced he would have tried to run her down.

"Don't you dare cry," he hissed as he put the car in drive. "Don't you dare."

But Claire couldn't stop. She was nearly hysterical. "Charles, please, please, *please* take me home. Please, Charles."

"I will if you won't tell."

Claire gritted her teeth and shook her head. Even now, her

tradition, her religious upbringing, her deep convictions told her that lying was wrong. "Of course I'm going to tell," Claire said. "Do you think I'm going to let you get away with this?"

"Then I'm not taking you home. And if you don't promise not to tell anyone, I'm gonna kill you."

So it had finally come to that. In a way, it had begun with a wedding and ended with a wedding. Claire's innocence had been bruised on a kitchen floor not even a week after her wedding gown had been stored away. Her dreams had been shattered by a fist that had come swinging through the panel of a locked front door. Her identity as a woman, a mother, and most of all, a wife, lay crumpled and cowering under the covers of a king-sized bed in the master bedroom. And now, after an unpleasant scene at a church wedding, Claire's very life was at stake, trembling and terrified, held hostage in the passenger seat of a Mercury Capri.

It lasted four hours. Four hours in the car, threatened, verbally abused, and beaten. Claire was the closest she had ever been to death at the hand of her husband. Each time Claire moved to open her door and get out, Charles would speed up. Even if she did get out, he'd grab her and haul her back in. Periodically he'd stop, reach over, grab her hair and punch her in the side, or choke her. Several times Claire nearly passed out because she simply could not breathe.

It isn't necessary to go into all the details here. What had happened before, happened now—only more severely. Charles wanted Claire to promise that she wouldn't tell anyone. Claire wouldn't promise any such thing. Charles would then beat her again. And the pattern would be repeated.

Once, Charles drove by the house to see if the kids were home. Mike's car was in the drive, and Charles sped right by.

Then Charles told Claire to straighten herself up. "Fix yourself so that we can meet Herb and Jean," he said.

"You've got to be kidding," Claire said through her tears and pain. "There's no way I can go now. No way."

"Sure you can. Just fix yourself up."

"I can't."

"You *can.* Fix yourself up. We'll have a nice evening."

Claire refused, and the pattern started again.

Claire prayed that Herb and Jean had started looking for

them. *Maybe they would've called Mike at home,* she thought without much hope.

Once, she did see the Simpsons' car entering the subdivision. But Herb and Jean didn't see the Capri, and Charles was able to elude them without much trouble.

Claire wondered if she would die right there in the car. As soon as the Simpsons were out of sight, Charles pulled over and tried to choke Claire again. He rammed her up against the car door until she was screaming and crying. He shouted, "If it hadn't been for you, this wouldn't have lasted so long! If you had just let me take you to the restaurant. . . ."

"Take me home, Charles. Please."

"Promise not to say anything to anyone."

"Yes, yes, *yes.* I promise."

"You won't tell?"

"No. I won't tell."

They went home, and Claire was able to crawl into bed without the kids seeing her. Charles had won. He had broken her. He had secured from her a promise he knew she would keep. He knew she wouldn't lie.

He was wrong.

> Daughter, your faith has made you well; go in peace.
> *Jesus, to the woman with an issue of blood.*
> (Luke 8:48, RSV)

Nine
Morning Has Broken

Sunday morning, Charles was up at the crack of dawn and fixed breakfast. Claire awoke to the smell of bacon sizzling downstairs, and remembered the terrifying events of the previous day. Actually, it was her aches and pains that prodded her recollections—in particular, soreness around her face and neck where she had been choked and a bruise along her side where she had been rammed into the door handle of the car.

Claire remembered her promise to herself: *One more physical incident, one more beating, no matter how trivial, will spell the end of the marriage.* And then she recalled her promise to Charles: *No, I won't tell anyone.* It wasn't even close. Getting out of bed that morning, Claire knew immediately which promise she would keep.

She went to the kitchen and told Charles that she was going to explain to the children what had happened.

"Don't do that, Claire," he said. "I swear I'll never do it again if you just won't tell. I swear it. You promised you wouldn't."

"And you promised a million times that you'd never touch me again. But you did, didn't you?"

"Yes, and I don't know why I do that. I'm sorry, Claire. I need you to forgive me and not be mad at me. Honey, please."

Claire shook her head. She gathered the kids together in Mike's room. Charles joined them, a pained expression on his face. He was still silently begging her not to do this.

Mike woke up, rubbed his eyes, and sat up in bed. Debbie stumbled in and sat on the floor. Her eyes were still half closed. Tricia was still asleep. She was too young to be a witness to this.

"I want you to know that your father beat me up," Claire said.

"I did not," Charles protested. "I didn't do anything. I—"

"He kept me in the car for four hours, pulling my hair, choking me, punching me, and threatening to kill me." She spoke softly and calmly. "I want you to see what your father did." She lifted her robe to show bruises up and down her legs and up the outside of her thighs. She showed the marks on her arms and told the kids how her face and neck hurt.

Mike slid down into the bed, turned away from the family and let his face sink into his pillow. He remembered his threat to kill his father if it ever happened again.

Charles's protests were by now more feeble. "I didn't. I swear," he said quietly.

"You did," Debbie responded quickly. "You should be in prison. If it happens again and Mother doesn't turn you in, I will."

Silence hung heavy. Nothing else was said. Charles walked out, leaving Claire and the children together. Debbie came over and put her arms around her. Mike groaned into his pillow.

Later that morning Charles reminded everyone that the family was expected at church for a family picture. It was a biennial activity of the church, a time when a photographer was hired and families could sign up for portraits to be taken.

"I'm not going," Debbie said. "No way. Not now."

But Claire talked her into it, assuring her that something would be done about the beatings. Claire would deal with the situation. "But we can't let it keep us from fulfilling our obligations. No matter what, we're still a family."

They missed church, but showed up for the photo session. They rode in separate cars. Charles walked in smiling from ear to ear, and he joked and laughed freely with some of the other men. Claire sat tight-lipped and stiff.

Photographs, especially portrait photos such as the one taken of Claire and her family that Sunday, derive their popularity from the fact that they tell lies about their subjects. They make people look better than they are. They fail to record the invisible: the troubles, pains, and emotions underneath a person's physical expression. In front of a camera, a person smiles, possibly despite a headache or an upset stomach or something deeper and painful in a different way: a feeling of inferiority, a flagging sense of worth, or an argument with a friend, relative, or spouse.

Claire's family managed smiles all around for their portrait that day, but looking closer you can see that the picture is lying. Claire's smile covers, of course, a great many physical pains, but something more as well—the beginnings of depression. Mike's smile is the most troubled—there is anger in his eyes—and Tricia's expression is the most natural, although perhaps her face betrays a trace of concern—she has sensed something. Debbie grins in a way that is at odds with her body language: she is holding her mother's hand and leaning into her slightly—the touch of empathy. Then Charles. His smile is the broadest of them all, but you can see it strain. He has forced it too far. And what you detect in the gaze of his eyes is, strangely, not rage, not anger, but confusion and desperation—the awful feeling that life has gone badly out of control and there's nothing to be done about it.

Getting out. Once Claire had made up her mind that she was going to leave, it was relatively easy for her to do so. It might seem heartless, after all that's gone before, for me to say that Claire had a lot going for her. But in a way she did. She had a career. She had friends and relatives nearby and a strong connection with a church fellowship. Furthermore, she was quite assured that her children were safe: Charles had never physically abused them, and Claire was convinced that he wouldn't in the future. Probably most important, Claire had a separate checking account. For Claire, leaving was as easy as walking out the front door.

For many women that's not the case. Jennifer Baker

Fleming, in her book, *Stopping Wife Abuse,* lists fourteen reasons why a woman stays with a man who has abused her. They include emotional dependence, economic dependence, low self-esteem, and isolation—characteristics that in combination can for some women make the prospect of walking out a Herculean act. And if children are in danger as well, matters are complicated even more; it's easier to find a place for a woman to live than for an entire family.

These are the realities of wife abuse in many situations across America. Still, the correct advice to battered women is this: *Walk out the front door.* Find a friend or relative to help you. Turn to the church if you can. Get to a hospital if you are hurt. Take the kids if they will be in danger. It's scary to step out into the world like that—but do it. Arrangements will be made; problems can be worked out later. *Seek safety first.*

What Claire did that next week serves as a fairly good model for any woman suffering from wife abuse and making the break from the home. In the process of leaving, Claire consulted the following people, in this order:

friends
doctor
parents
pastor
lawyer
counselor

Of course, each woman's situation is different. But some general advice can be given which should apply in any case. It is essential for a battered woman to inform other people what has been going on. Hiding the truth in an effort to protect the husband or to avoid personal embarrassment does no good. It doesn't help the batterer and it certainly doesn't help the victim. Also, it is wise for an abused wife or battered woman to seek immediate medical attention even if the injuries seem relatively mild. A doctor's examination not only can help discover more serious internal injuries that might otherwise go undetected but also can provide the written, professional verification of the nature of the abuse. This is often helpful in a legal situation, but is also proof positive to the woman herself and to her parents and friends that abuse has occurred.

Again, Claire's actions happen to be a good model. This is what Claire did, and here is how it happened.

Sunday

After the family portrait was taken, Charles spent the rest of the day pleading with Claire to forgive him. She could tell he was primarily concerned about her going to a lawyer or telling anyone else about what happened. She made only one promise. "You can go to work without any fears of being exposed," she said. "I won't ruin your career."

Monday

In the morning Claire had a doctor's appointment, one that had been scheduled a long time before. It was to be a routine visit, but now it took on added significance. Claire's bruises were showing deep purple. Her aches and pains, especially around her neck had gotten worse, not better, the second day after the beating.

Charles was astonished to hear that Claire was going to keep the appointment. "You're still going to the doctor?" he asked. He had put on his charming personality since Saturday, but now, upon hearing this news, he raised his voice slightly, and an edge of fear and defensiveness crept into his tone. "You're going looking like that?"

"You bet I am," Claire replied firmly.

What Charles didn't realize was that as long as he kept his mouth shut, Claire actually felt sorry for him. But when he spoke up, raised his voice, or tried to cover himself, she felt disgusted, and she became even more resolved to act strongly.

"Are you gonna tell him?" Charles was anxious to know.

"He'll ask."

"Let me go with you. I'll tell him."

"Sure you will," Claire replied sarcastically.

"Yeah. I'll tell him. Really."

"And exactly *what* will you tell him?" Claire's voice trembled. She paused to gain control, then said bitterly, "What will you make up this time?"

"No stories. I'll tell the truth."

"This I've gotta see."

Charles surprised her. He went with her. He told the doctor he had lost his temper and would never do it again. The doctor was a member of the school board and thus happened to be a friend of Charles's from their monthly school board meetings.

"People can do a lot of things in a fit of rage," the doctor said. He prescribed something for Charles that would help calm him down.

Tuesday

The next morning Claire awoke to the sound of rain pattering against the windowpanes in the bedroom. As she lay in bed, she realized that it might be her last time in that room.

Everyone had left the house—the kids had made it to school and Charles had an hour before gone to work. Claire was alone. She found herself luxuriating in the dark, soft comfort of her bedroom, the rain providing a light sleepy rhythm for the morning. It felt so good to allow herself to sink into the mattress, to soothe those muscles that ached from bruises and tension, that she giggled and then started to laugh. In a minute the laughter changed into sobs, and Claire cried until her pillowcase was wet with her tears.

Later she fixed a breakfast of grapefruit and toast. Her mind was filling up with things she needed to do. "First things first," she said to herself. She sighed as she sat beside the telephone.

She told her parents everything. Of course, they had known about some of it, but they had believed that matters were improving. This news shocked and scared them.

"You've got to get out, Claire," her father said. "You've *got* to this time."

"I will, Dad," Claire replied.

"Right away?"

"Yes, tonight."

"Have you been to a doctor? Are you all right?"

"Yes. Yes, I'm OK."

"Honey, you can stay here with us."

Claire reached for a Kleenex in her purse. "Thanks, Dad. I will. But tonight I'm staying with Suzanne. From church. You don't know her. But she's sweet. She offered."

"Then she knows?"

"Sort of. Yes, I guess so."

Claire's father paused at the other end of the line. "This is awful," he said, almost to himself. "How do things go so wrong?"

"I don't know, Dad." A sob rose up in Claire's throat. "I've got to go."

"Are you working today?"

"No. But I want to. Need to. For myself, I think, not for the work. I'll talk with you tomorrow."

"Your mother and I love you. Make sure you're safe."

As Claire hung up and as fresh tears started to flow, she saw more clearly why she felt like getting back to work, despite all that happened. She didn't want to drop out of life. She wanted to drop out of Charles's life.

Late Tuesday afternoon, Claire went to the office to tell one other friend, Maxine, what had happened.

"I never imagined—" Maxine started to say.

"I didn't let anyone imagine it," Claire replied.

It was the end of the business day and the other employees had already cleared out. Maxine and Claire locked up and headed out to the parking lot. The rain, which had been off and on all day, was now a downpour. They ran back into the office to scrounge up some umbrellas. Suddenly Claire got the feeling that Charles was nearby.

"You're kidding," Maxine said.

"No. I'm sure of it. He's here."

They didn't find umbrellas, but they covered their heads with newspapers and dashed out into the rain.

Charles was running toward them. "Claire!" he called.

He, of course, was Mr. Jovial. He had no idea that Maxine knew the whole story. "I was just checking to make sure you were all right in the rain."

"I've survived rain before," Claire said, coldly.

Charles laughed.

Maxine scowled.

The three of them were getting drenched. "Here," Charles said, "Let me walk you to the car."

Maxine waited for Claire to say something, but Claire didn't. She suddenly seemed lifeless, defeated. Charles took

Claire's arm, and they walked away. "Good night, Maxine," Charles called over his shoulder.

"Good night," Maxine replied. She walked off toward her blue Mustang, glancing back to make sure Claire was safe.

Charles used his keys to open Claire's car door. She was petrified. Charles sat inside with her. In the back were piles of Claire's clothing. "Where the ——— are you going with that?"

"I'm leaving, Charles."

"What do you mean?"

"I mean what I said. I'm leaving. It's not so hard to figure out."

Charles renewed his promises and again begged her to stay.

"Tonight," Claire said, "I'm going to Suzanne's."

Charles panicked. "Then everyone will know."

"That's all you care about."

"Of course not." But Charles stopped protesting. He had heard himself, his own words. He knew it was true. He was thinking about himself, his career, his friends in the community who would now find out. They would *know*. He tried again—"Just don't go to Suzanne's. Not there, Honey"—but it was a feeble attempt at forestalling the inevitable.

"I'm going," Claire said. "Suzanne already knows anyway. It's done."

Charles followed Claire to Suzanne's. What neither realized was that Maxine was following too. She didn't trust Charles and was concerned for Claire's safety.

Suzanne had been waiting for Claire, periodically looking out the window for her car. When Claire pulled into the drive, Suzanne noticed another car slow down in front of the house. The streetlamp cast its yellow beam across the face of the car's driver. It was Charles. Suzanne immediately flipped on the switch to the outside floodlight which bathed the whole front yard and drive in brightness. Charles drove off, Suzanne opened her front door, and Claire climbed out of the car.

No one saw, a moment later, a blue Mustang cruise by slowly, and then head for home.

Wednesday

By Wednesday morning Claire's sharper pains had subsided but many of her aches and sorenesses persisted. When she awoke at nine it took her nearly a minute to orient herself to her new surroundings. She had slept well and deeply; even so, she was exhausted when she awoke. She wanted to stay in bed for another eight or nine hours.

But Claire knew she couldn't. She had business to attend to. First, she would call her pastor. He had been a close friend and had been very supportive of her in the past. She told him everything.

The Rev. James Cranston was shocked. He had had no idea.

"What are you going to do?" he asked.

"I'm going to the lawyer tomorrow."

"I see." Cranston tried quickly to think through the situation. What does a pastor do or say in such a situation? Cranston was new to the pastorate, and at thirty-five was relatively young and inexperienced. He was a dynamic preacher, and the small congregation liked that very much. He would draw outsiders into the church. He was very personable on a one-to-one basis, and Jim and Shirley, his wife of two years, were highly involved in the congregation's and the community's social life. But one of the things Jim Cranston found difficult was pastoral counseling. He knew he had much to learn about people's problems. He needed experience. Being a man of self-motivation and action, Cranston decided to grab as much experience as he could get by facing head on those personal and marital problems that came to him. When before he had tended to refer those people to outside counselors, now he took them himself, shepherding them into his pastor's office with his left hand and wielding the wisdom of the Scriptures with his right.

"I have a business acquaintance who is a fine lawyer," Claire was saying.

"Claire," Pastor Jim said, "do you think that's wise?"

"What do you mean?"

"Well, I mean we all tend to make unfortunate decisions when we're upset." The pastor groped for the right words. "It would be too bad if you started something that was irreversible. I just hope you won't do anything rash."

"Rash?"

"Marriage is a precious thing, Claire."

"It seems to me that it's had its chance."

"Well, yes." Pastor Jim paused, choosing his words carefully. He knew this sort of thing went on—wife abuse—but he had never before encountered it personally. They hadn't taught it in seminary. "Claire," he said, "whatever you do, make sure you tell your lawyer that his job, and my job, is to save marriages."

Claire was stunned. Had she not told him of all that had gone on for eighteen years of marriage? Did he need an entire blow-by-blow account of the hundreds of beatings through the years? Did he really think Claire was giving up on this marriage too soon?

Suddenly Claire felt something in addition to her aches and intense exhaustion.

Guilt.

Thursday

She did go to the lawyer on Thursday, but she went to the doctor first—this time a different doctor.

Actually, Dr. Victor Franz had been Claire's regular doctor for more than fifteen years. Two years earlier, Franz had gone overseas on a leave of absence. Claire had found another doctor—Charles's friend on the school board—and had grown accustomed to him. Meanwhile Dr. Franz returned and resumed his practice. It now seemed appropriate to Claire, especially after seeing her other doctor and Charles shake hands after the examination on Monday, that she should go back to Dr. Franz.

There was another reason why Claire returned to him. Franz was aware of the abuse. Claire had never said anything about the beatings, but she knew she didn't have to. Dr. Franz could see what was going on. He knew, and she knew he knew. And nothing was ever said.

Dr. Franz was a gruff, cold man in his late fifties and a lot of people didn't like him. He was, however, reputed the best doctor in town, and so many community members put up with his chilly personality.

During the fifteen years Claire had gone to Franz, she had grown to appreciate his expertise. He was thorough and he seemed to understand her. Claire wondered if he was that way with every patient, or just her. Still he never said much, and he always wore a scowl. He was a hard man to like.

And when Claire entered the examination room this summer Thursday at ten-thirty, Dr. Franz showed no sign of recognizing her. It had been two years, Claire realized, but she had hoped for a warmer welcome.

The examination took twenty-five minutes. Dr. Franz left the room and Claire dressed. When he returned, he sat down and studied the copious notes he had jotted down. Presently, he looked up at Claire. She saw something in his eyes she had never seen before. For the first time ever, Franz called her by her first name.

"Claire," he said, "these beatings are getting much worse. You need to protect yourself."

"I have left him," Claire replied simply.

The elderly Dr. Franz nodded and looked down at his clipboard of notes. As he turned to leave the examination room, he muttered, in such a way that Claire barely heard him. "I'm very glad."

"Unfortunately, the legal system is designed to protect the batterer—the husband—not the abused wife," the lawyer told Claire later that day. "If your husband had done the same thing to a stranger, he would have been arrested and put in prison for assault and battery. But you're his wife. According to the law, you have very few rights."

"How come?" Claire asked. "It just doesn't seem fair."

"It's *not* fair. It's grossly unjust."

"Then why is it set up that way?"

"Two reasons," the young lawyer said. He spoke with a kind of certainty—even arrogance. "First, it's traditional. For centuries the legal system has extended to husbands what is called 'the right of chastisement' over their wives. Laws have changed in the last hundred or so years, sure. But attitudes haven't. Second, the law is reluctant to get involved in situations occurring inside the home. Nobody wants a government that intrudes upon the family."

"I don't want to put Charles in prison," Claire said. "I just want to keep him away from me."

"Even that's hard to do. Well, we can accomplish it *legally*. We can make it illegal for him to bother you. But that in itself may not keep him from doing so."

"But, if he did bother me, and if it were illegal, could he be arrested?"

"Maybe. But that's up to the police. The police are very reluctant to get involved in domestic squabbles. In fact, that's how cops get killed. A lot of them. Fights between a husband and wife."

Claire shook her head. "You're not giving me a lot of hope."

The lawyer smiled and said, "There's not much to give. Those are the facts of life."

Claire looked at him from the other side of his immense mahogany desk. He was young, maybe twenty-nine, attractive, with sandy-colored hair, blue eyes and fair skin. He was a pleasant fellow, although a little cocky perhaps. Claire could forgive that in someone so young. Mike would be like that someday.

Suddenly Claire felt old. She was only thirty-five, but she felt more like fifty. This young lawyer was already successful. He seemed happy and prosperous—and he still had a lifetime ahead of him. Claire wondered why her life had to be so different from his. She recalled what her father had said. *How do things go so wrong?* She thought about all the choices she had made that had led to this. How long had it taken to make those choices? A second? A minute? Five minutes to make the choices that ruined an entire lifetime? *How long had it taken to decide to marry Charles?*

Claire looked straight at the young lawyer who had so many choices left to make, so many opportunities, and said, "I've made all my choices. They're all gone."

Tears rolled down her cheeks, and the young lawyer quickly and awkwardly reached for his handkerchief. His composure, that dashing certainty about him, suddenly broke. He fumbled the handkerchief and it fell on the desk. He retrieved it and held it out to Claire. He looked foolish now, uncomfortable in the presence of tears.

Claire took his handkerchief and dabbed at her eyes. "Thanks," she said. "I'm sorry. This has been happening a lot."

The lawyer nodded. He turned away from her and picked up a file.

Claire went on. "But it's true, isn't it? In this situation—legally, I mean—I don't have many choices."

The lawyer glanced over at Claire, saw that she had composed herself, then turned to face her. "There's always divorce," he said.

"There's always divorce," Claire repeated slowly.

"It's up to you." The lawyer faced Claire once again, regaining his composure. He sounded cocky again and a little condescending.

"I was told to tell you something," Claire said. "My pastor wants you to know that it's your business and his to save marriages."

The young lawyer smiled. He welcomed the challenge. "I would think," he said, "that it would be your pastor's job to save *souls.*"

Friday

Each day of the week Claire had checked on the kids. They seemed to handle the situation well. *Kids,* Claire thought, *seem to adjust so well. But what effects will this have on their lives?*

Claire wanted to make sure the girls were safe. Mike could take care of himself. He could continue to live at home with Charles, although he avoided his father as much as possible. Debbie had arranged to stay at a friend's house indefinitely. Claire called to make sure it was OK and to offer to pay for room and board. The offer was refused. "It's the least we can do," was the reply. Claire hadn't told them the exact problem, hinting only that there had been some troubles at home. She wondered how much Debbie had said. Claire realized that eventually a lot of people would know. But she couldn't worry about keeping up appearances any longer.

Claire's sister offered to take eleven-year-old Tricia. It was a good solution. There she would be close to school and to her friends.

Friday afternoon, while Charles was still away at work, Claire picked up Tricia at home to drop her off at her sister's house. On the way, Tricia asked, "Will you and Daddy ever get married again?"

"But, honey," Claire replied, "we *are* married."

"Yeah," Tricia said, sliding over beside her mother, "but you don't *live* married."

Saturday

Saturday, of course, was the one-week "anniversary" of the severe beating. It wasn't the sort of anniversary you'd want to remember, much less, celebrate. But Claire wasn't allowed to forget. That night she began having the nightmares that would plague her for months. They would terrify her and wake her in the middle of the night, depriving her of precious sleep.

Charles was in the dreams, and he was trying to kill her.

> Jesus said to his mother, "Woman, behold, your son!" Then he said to the disciple, "Behold, your mother!"
> *Jesus, to Mary, his mother, and John*
> (John 19:26, 27, RSV)

Ten
Falling Apart into Wholeness

Mrs. Olson: Do you think you're getting better?
Claire: It helps talking through this.
Mrs. Olson: How does it help? Do you feel better?
Claire: No. I *feel* worse. But somehow I sense that I'm *getting* better.
Mrs. Olson: When you first came, you were depressed. Are you still depressed, Claire?
Claire: No. Now I feel angry.
Mrs. Olson: Whom are you angry with?
Claire: Charles, of course.
Mrs. Olson: No one else?
Claire: No. Who else would there be?

The events of Claire's story can be reported to you chronologically; the healing that took place cannot. I had seen some changes in Claire—in her personality, in her physical presence, even in the way she dressed—that were clues pointing to the healing inside her. Often these clues were imperceptible, even to me, but taken together were quite noticeable.

This reminds me of a motion picture I saw, a fantasy or fairy story of some kind, in which a plain, homely girl was, by the magic of a wand, transformed into a beautiful princess. The special effects were so subtly controlled and slow that you could hardly discern the specific facial changes on the screen. But then, sure enough, after a minute or so the transformation had occurred, and the girl had become a lovely young princess.

Every so often in my sessions with Claire I'd be reminded of that motion picture. I would look up from my notes and see across from me a different Claire than the one who had first come to visit me only months before. The changes, little healings, occurred slowly and imperceptibly. But at certain times I would notice a new Claire, or *newer* Claire; the accumulation of all those minute, subtle changes would have a total effect that was sometimes stunning.

That is why healing is a difficult thing to write about. I wish therapy was as easy and as dramatic as waving a wand over someone's head. But, of course, there are no wands. And you can't write special effects into a book.

So, exactly when or how the healing took place in Claire's life, I can't tell you. It certainly didn't happen at any one time—some colossal moment of self-realization. And it didn't even happen in a series of life-changing events. Claire was still curled up in her fears and defenses. "Do you believe God loves you?" was the question she still couldn't answer. But I could tell that God was holding Claire as a mother holds her newborn, and that he was gently showing her those things she had cried out for for so long—life and hope and, above all, love.

My good friend Dr. Franz and I kept close contact concerning Claire and her progress. Despite the grim demeanor he always sported in public, he really cared deeply about his patients and especially about Claire. Over the months he and I shared many phone conversations together. One in particular seemed to shed as much light on him as it did on Claire—a most interesting dialogue.

That Thursday after the beating in the car, Franz had counted some thirty-four visible bruises on Claire's body. "That's not to mention those things that a physician can't see," he said. "She must have been in a great deal of pain.

"I hadn't seen her—oh, for maybe a year or so—she had gone to someone else. So I was surprised she had come back.

But I have notes in my files going back fifteen years describing her condition. Each time it was abuse—I'm sure of it."

"How do you feel when you see this kind of thing? I sure can tell you how *I* feel."

"Yes, I know. I see the outside hurts. You see the inside hurts. You get angry, don't you? I have no compassion for the husband. Whatever he's facing, no matter what pressures he's under—there's no excuse. It's brutality, Esther."

"I know."

"She has a kid doesn't she—a boy?"

"Three children. Mike's eighteen or so."

"Well, I think Mike ought to go and break the guy's jaw, if he's big and tough enough to do it. There's nothing like a broken jaw for involuntary therapy."

"I work a little less violently, you know."

"I know. I just get frustrated with this business because I can't do anything about it. If you have appendicitis, I take out your appendix. There's a problem, and I have a solution. But with this sort of thing—I don't know. I don't have a feeling for it. That's why I referred Claire to you."

"I think you do have a feeling for it."

"For the victim, maybe. It's the abuser I don't understand."

Dr. Franz also said he saw numerous cases of wife abuse, and that the problem seemed to be increasing. Few, however, had such a long history as Claire.

The nightmares Claire had were signs of healing. They were also signs of pain—emotional pain that would now surface after being repressed for so many years. Perhaps it seems Claire had now been through the worst of it. In fact, she was just beginning to experience the emotional and psychological abuse that had for so long taken a back seat to the physical. It is essential to understand this to understand Claire. Wife abuse was not, as Charles thought, a faucet you could turn off; the problem could not be fixed so simply as saying, "I'm sorry. It will never happen again," *even if it never did recur*—because the abuse rages on within the woman for years and years after she is safe and free. As was said at the beginning of this book, wife abuse does not leave just facial scars and thigh bruises. It assaults the very identity of a woman and subverts her own sense of what she is and what she can be. That's the horror of wife abuse, and it goes far to explain the kind of torment Claire still had to endure.

Phillip Yancey, in his book *Where Is God When It Hurts?*, argues that pain is a gift from God. This is hard to understand, especially when you're the one who's suffering. The natural response is to ask, "Why, God? Why make me go through this?" But it's more easily grasped when you come face to face with people who feel no pain—as Yancey did—people who suffer from Hansen's disease, better known as leprosy. These people, without the gift of pain, are subject to all kinds of debilitating injuries and diseases and cannot protect themselves because they never have any indication of when their bodies are being hurt. Yancey points out an interesting irony here: ours is a nation of people trying to escape pain—through all manner of pills and medications, including massive everyday use of aspirin and Tylenol and Tagamet—and here are the people who have "achieved" our goal—pain-free lives—and they happen to be lepers.

I think there is yet another angle to this. Just as so many of us try to rid ourselves of physical pain, so many of us also try to attain a pain-free emotional life. Perhaps we, like Claire, have been hurt so many times that we seek ways to avoid that pain, that emotional anguish which torments us. There are such people who have in some way attained that goal; they do not experience emotional pain—in fact, they do not experience emotion. They have become unfeeling. They have become emotional lepers.

There were times when Claire would realize more fully the depth of her hurts, the extent of the injuries Charles had inflicted upon her spirit. She would cry and sob, and her body would shake with emotional pain. It was hard to watch her that way, but I knew it was a gift from God. It was the pain of healing.

And later Claire and I would kneel in prayer. And I would praise God that Claire, despite all she'd been through, had not become an emotional leper. She was still a feeling person.

Claire: I had been gone for two weeks. Charles had talked to me on the phone. He wanted to see me. He wanted me to come back. I said no. I was very concerned about the kids. At one point I thought I really had ruined them by moving out. I felt so guilty.

Mrs. Olson: But it wasn't your fault.

Claire: No it wasn't. I *knew* that; I just didn't *feel* it. My mind told me it wasn't my fault. My heart kept whispering to me, "You've really done it this time. Now you've really messed up."

Two and a half weeks after Claire left Charles, she was back at the insurance company, working long hours. She would come in at six in the morning and leave late at night. For Claire, the job was a means of escape, a way to avoid loneliness.

One day, Claire looked up from her desk to see her son Mike leaning against the door to her office.

"Got time to talk?" he asked.

They had lunch at a deli around the corner. "It's hard work," Mike said after they had ordered sandwiches. He was speaking of his new landscaping job. "But for the summer it'll work out OK. I like the pay."

"Will you earn enough for school?" Claire wanted to know. Mike had just graduated from high school and was planning to enter college in the fall. He still hadn't made up his mind whether he'd go to the community college in town or to a school in Colorado. Either way, he'd need money. Claire had already promised to him a third of his support, and he could secure loans for another third. That left nearly $2,000 for him to raise himself.

"Yeah, I'll have enough."

Claire looked across the table at her son's tired eyes. "Are you sleeping at all?"

"Not much."

"Maybe you should see a doctor. He could prescribe something."

"I'll be OK, Mom."

The waitress came with their sandwiches and Cokes. When she had left, Mike spoke cautiously. "I've been reading a book."

"Oh? What's that?"

"It's a book on violence."

"Is that what you wanted to talk to me about?"

"No, I didn't want to talk to you about anything. I just wanted to talk, you know?"

Claire smiled. "Yes, I know. We need to do this more often. I worry about you."

Mike shook his head. "I worry about me, too," he said.

"So what's the book telling you?"

"That if I get married I might be likely to beat up on my wife because of what Dad did to you."

Claire looked up from her sandwich. Mike stared back at her through misty eyes. She could see he was scared. Claire thought of all that Mike had been through. He had suffered more than the other children. He had seen more of the violence than the others. It was Mike who had threatened to kill Charles, but then couldn't follow through on it. That, Claire knew, had troubled Mike immensely. That was why he couldn't get any sleep in the same house with his father—not because of what he was afraid he might do to Charles, but because of what he knew he wouldn't do. And now Mike had discovered something new that horrified him as much as if he has just learned that he had cancer—a propensity to violence. All of those traits Mike despised in his father, he was now told, could be reborn in him given the right circumstances.

Mike, trying not to cry, said, "I don't want to be like him."

"Oh, Mike, you won't be. You aren't anything like him. You don't care about money or being popular or owning beautiful cars. You care about people. You're kind, generous, eager to help, even when it means sacrifice. There isn't a trace of your father's behavior in you, and you can't let yourself think that even for a second. You've been wonderful to me—that should say something in itself. Forget what the book said."

"I can't. It's in my head."

"Michael, this isn't your problem. Don't take responsibility for it."

"But, Mom, I feel so guilty."

Claire reached across the table and placed her hand on his. "I know. I feel guilty too."

Mike quickly looked up at her, in his eyes the tears that he had tried so hard to control. "Why should *you* feel guilty?" he asked.

"I don't know. But it's the same with you. Why should *you* feel guilty?"

"*Because I didn't stop it.*" Mike's face contorted in an effort to hold back his emotions. His eyes closed tight, and he looked away.

Claire got up from her side of the table and sat next to Mike, putting her arm around his broad shoulders. He was such a big, strong boy, and yet he was breaking apart inside. "It's good to cry sometimes," Claire said, holding him. "We'll be OK, you and me. Put your head on my shoulder."

Mike shook his head. "Not here. We're in a restaurant."

"It's OK. I'm your mother."

Through his tears, Mike laughed. "I know. That's what I mean. It doesn't look good, you know? I'm practically an adult."

Claire smiled. "Michael, you *are* an adult," she said softly. "And there isn't an ounce of violence in you. In this case, the book is wrong."

Mike closed his eyes and leaned his head on her shoulder.

Mrs. Olson: Are you angry at God, Claire?
Claire: No.
Mrs. Olson: Are you sure?
Claire: Why should I be angry at God?
Mrs. Olson: Why are you so hostile?
Claire: I don't like the question.

Three weeks after she had left Charles, Claire received a phone call from the Rev. James Cranston.

"I want to know if you'll meet with me. And Charles."

"No," Claire replied immediately.

"I think it's important that you talk together."

"What good will it do?"

"It might show you how Charles has changed."

"Oh, I see," Claire said angrily, "he's conned you now, too."

"No, he hasn't conned me at all. I'm not taking sides in this, Claire. I just want you two to talk."

"I don't like it."

"There's no commitment in it, Claire. You don't have to go back with him. Just talk together."

After another ten minutes of conversation, the Rev. Cranston had convinced Claire. They would meet Thursday night at seven.

Claire: Why are you pressing me on this?
Mrs. Olson: Because I think you're angry at God, and I think you need to face that fact.
Claire: I'm not, though. You're fishing.
Mrs. Olson: Maybe. But you *are* angry.
Claire: I'm angry at Charles.
Mrs. Olson: I don't think so.
Claire: (Raising her voice.) How do you know? What makes you think you know me so well?
Mrs. Olson: You *should* be mad at Charles, but you're mad at God instead.
Claire: (Nervously.) This isn't getting us anywhere.
Mrs. Olson: I'm on to it, aren't I? Why, then? Why are you mad at God?

After a month, it was clear that Charles was no danger to the children. Over the phone Claire had agreed with Charles that it was best for the children to be at home. Claire was concerned about Debbie, particularly, because the family with whom she had been staying had noticed that Debbie had become more and more withdrawn, sometimes spending an entire day in her bedroom. Tricia and Debbie moved back home.

These kinds of problems, with both Mike and Debbie, only contributed to the load of guilt that Claire already carried. At night Claire would lie in bed exhausted, yet unable to sleep. She'd think over and over about what an awful mother she was. *If I were a good mother,* Claire would think, *I would grab up the kids and take them away from here. We'd set up a new home somewhere and I would give each of them all my time.* And then Claire would realize what folly that all was. She didn't have the strength to do all of that, and she was so terribly confused.

Tricia was the bright spot in Claire's life. As a seventh-grader, Tricia was growing up to be a sweet, attractive girl. She was bright and happy, and she was becoming very popular with school friends. Tricia seemed to adapt well to new situations; Claire never worried about her. And the thing that really cheered Claire was Tricia's outspoken love for Jesus. Sometimes Tricia talked with her mother over the phone about something she had read in her Bible, and Tricia would sound so radiant and enthused by the Scripture that Claire would envy the innocence and freshness of her Christian walk. The two developed an unusual relationship during those days. And a careful observer would understand that it was the spiritual strength of the daughter that helped the mother persevere.

Mrs. Olson: God didn't cause you to suffer, Claire. You've got to come to see that.
Claire: I'm not saying he did.
Mrs. Olson: Then what is this anger? Where is it coming from?
Claire: (No response.)
Mrs. Olson: Why are you hiding this? You've been so open with me, Claire.
Claire: (No response.)
Mrs. Olson: I can't help you then.
Claire: (No response.)
Mrs. Olson: You may as well pack up and go home. I can't help you.
Claire: (Her voice trembling.) OK, I'll tell you. But I'm ashamed to say it.

Thursday evening at seven o'clock, Claire walked into the pastor's study to see the Rev. Cranston and Charles sitting there chatting. They both stood as Claire entered. Charles held out his hand to help Claire to the chair next to his; she chose instead to sit in the leather chair beside the door.

"I'm glad you came," said the pastor, smiling. "I had my doubts you would show."

"I did too," Claire replied grimly, "until an hour or so ago."

Charles said nothing, but sat nodding and smiling. Whenever Claire looked over at him, he looked back wearing that fake grin of his. A part of Claire felt sorry for him: she knew how much it was hurting him to air all of this in front of the pastor. She knew that Charles's smile was a valiant attempt to cover that hurt.

At the same time, every look at Charles brought to Claire a feeling of revulsion, a reminder of violence and pain. She remembered her disgust at Charles's constant efforts to maneuver, to get the best deal for himself, and to look out for himself at the expense of everyone else.

Pastor Cranston spoke. "It's my job to bring you together. I feel there is hope for your marriage. I think maybe something can be accomplished by you two talking this thing over. Now if ever I'm in the way, just let me know, and I'll leave. I don't need to be in on everything—or anything, for that matter. At first, I'll just be a kind of moderator; someone needs to regulate the conversation, to keep it fair and honest. But, again—and I want to make this clear—I'm quite dispensable to this process. Whenever you want me to leave, just let me know."

"I want you to stay," Claire said firmly. "It's not always safe for me in the presence of Charles."

"Why don't we talk about that, Claire?" Cranston said. "Tell me about what's happened."

For the next forty-five minutes Claire laid out a picture of the marriage—the story of the abuse, the finances, Charles's lists, the impact on the children, etc. Claire spoke slowly and deliberately, never once looking at Charles. Charles remained silent except for one time when he mumbled, "It wasn't like that." Claire plunged ahead through the story, at times detailing the beatings she suffered.

When she was done, Charles sat shaking his head. Pastor Cranston remained silent, leaning back in his chair, looking straight at Claire. He turned to Charles. "Chuck," he said, "what do you say to this?"

Charles leaned forward and spoke in a low, controlled voice. "I'll be the first to say that I've done some wrong things. I've done some bad things in my life. The last few days talking with you, Jim, have made me see myself in a new way. Well, I'll admit all of that. But I don't think that whatever I did to

Claire was ever that bad. It just wasn't that bad. Not the way she says. How could I ever do things like that?"

"But you *did*," Claire interrupted. "Too many people know for you to deny this—your parents, my parents, the kids, my doctor. *You did it!*"

"But not that way."

"Two people can look at the same thing and receive two different impressions of it," Cranston said. "Both of you may be right—each in a different way."

"But, pastor," Claire protested, "Charles didn't just slap me a few times. He nearly killed me!"

"I don't doubt that these—these incidents—seemed, shall we say, life-threatening."

"They didn't just seem life-threatening. They *were* life-threatening! He tried to kill me—several times."

"I did not," Charles said.

"Call the doctor. Call my parents. Call *your* parents, Charles. They'll tell you the same thing."

The two were shouting now, and the Rev. Cranston had to raise his voice to gain control of the situation. "Does it really matter," he asked rhetorically, "exactly what happened and how it happened? The question is, 'Will it happen again?' I have reason to believe that it won't."

To Claire it seemed as if the two—Charles and the pastor—had already come to some kind of agreement between them. Claire felt cornered.

The pastor leaned forward and folded his hands on top of his desk. He spoke directly to Claire in a low soothing voice. "I have been made aware," he said, "that Charles has been under a great deal of pressure. There has been a decline of enrollment in the school system; budget cuts have taken their toll on the educational system; the number of people seeking a job—Charles's job—in the school system has doubled in the last few years. Charles has, as you must know, been working long, long hours—"

"But that doesn't give him the right to beat his wife," Claire interrupted.

"No, of course not. But it helps us understand how it might happen. Charles says the situation has turned around now. The pressure is not as great. Is that right, Charles?"

Charles nodded. "It's different now," he said. "Honey, I swear it'll be different."

"What'll be different?" Claire asked. "What do you think is going to happen?"

"I want you to come back to me. I need you."

Claire couldn't reply. She turned away from him.

"I think I'd better make something clear," Cranston said. "The Bible says that marriage is sacred. I have a duty—you, Claire, and you, Charles, have a duty also—to see that everything possible is done to preserve this marriage."

Claire shook her head. "I've been through this before," she said. "He's promised to change before. It never happened."

"It will happen, honey."

"What's different?" Claire snapped. "What possibly could change you so much now that couldn't change you for all these years? Do you think that my moving out on you has had that much of an effect? I doubt it. I really do doubt it. It'll all be the same if I move back. It'll happen all over again."

Pastor Cranston spoke up. "Something has changed," he said. There was an eagerness in his voice that he could barely restrain. Charles, this is yours to tell."

Claire looked over at Charles. A smile spread over his face. He possessed a different presence, it seemed. Claire had never seen him this way before.

"It happened Monday night," he said. "Right here in this study. I've been saved, Claire. I'm a Christian now."

Claire: (In a loud voice.) *Yes!* I admit it. I *am* angry at God!

Mrs. Olson: Say it again.

Claire: I'm angry at God.

Mrs. Olson: Why are you angry at God? Because he caused you to suffer?

Claire: No.

Mrs. Olson: Claire. Open up. Say it. Do you think God caused your suffering?

Claire: No. He didn't make me suffer. God didn't do that. Charles did.

Mrs. Olson: Then why are you angry at God?

Claire: Because Charles became a Christian.

> "Please give me a drink,"
> Jesus said to her. . . .
> The Samaritan woman
> said to him, "How can you,
> a Jew, ask for a drink from
> me, a woman of Samaria?"
> (For Jews have no
> dealings with Samaritans.)
> "If you knew what God
> can give," Jesus replied,
> "and if you knew who it is
> that said to you, 'Give me
> a drink,' you would have
> asked him, and he would
> have given you living water."
> *Jesus and the woman at the well*
> (John 4:7-10, Phillips)

Eleven
The Homecoming

Claire stood inside the airport terminal and peered through the big window, across the landing field, and into the fields beyond. It was late Wednesday evening—nearly a week after the meeting with the pastor and Charles. Darkness had fallen, but there was still a streak of purple slashing across the sky at the horizon. For once in this unusually wet month of August, there was no rain. For once in Claire's stormy life there were no tears. Everything had dried up.

Mike sat in one of the orange molded plastic chairs with his back to the window. His face was pressed into his hands and he was bent over.

The two were waiting for the Pan Am flight from Chicago to taxi in from the runway. Claire held a ticket for the return trip. She'd stay a few days in Chicago with friends. She needed time to think.

Mike stood up and said, "I'm gonna get a hot dog. Want something?"

Claire shook her head.

Alone now, but for the straggle of passengers walking through the corridor, Claire reflected on the events of the past week. Charles's conversion had suddenly put Claire in a bind. She couldn't deny the possibility that indeed he had become a Christian and changed. It was, after all, with that hope she had married him. But the timing was all wrong. It seemed suspicious, and Claire wondered if this might not just be another of Charles's ploys, a clever device contrived to get her back.

It was a Catch-22: if Claire didn't give Charles another chance, it would be an admission that she didn't have faith in God to change him; if she did go back with him, she could well be placing herself back in the danger from which she had just narrowly escaped.

To complicate matters, the pastor had emerged squarely on Charles's side. Oh, he had been diplomatic, and he had pretended to remain neutral, but by the time Claire had gotten up out of that leather lounger and had prepared to leave, it was clear that the pastor wanted Claire to return to Charles. He left with her the impression that if she didn't she was being unreasonable and unforgiving.

It was evident that the pastor never really did understand the problem. Pastor Cranston never really grasped the idea that this was more than a domestic argument, that Charles had nearly killed her. The two men had drawn up, right in front of Claire that evening in the pastor's study, a list of promises and conditions—a contract—which would oblige Charles to treat Claire properly. It included everything—from not swearing to taking Claire out once a week. Claire thought it ridiculous and said so. "If he hasn't kept his marriage vows," she had said, "what makes you think he'll live up to this silly contract?" But the two continued writing it up. They had finished with a flourish, like a couple of used car salesmen working up a deal. Then Pastor Cranston turned to Claire and said, "Well, how about it? Give Charles another chance."

She should have said no. But Claire had mumbled, "I'll think about it," and then she left.

For some reason, the airport was quiet this Wednesday night. Claire watched as the trucks and service vans scurried underneath the 727, preparing the plane for takeoff. Mike had returned, having polished off two hot dogs and a Coke. *At least his appetite is still healthy,* Claire thought. But he had sat back down, solemn and troubled. Claire knew that with Mike it wasn't depression as it was with Debbie, but it was worry—about the family and about himself.

"Will you be OK?" Claire asked.

"Don't worry about me." Mike stared at the floor.

"But I do."

"Yeah, I know." Mike stood, stuffed his hands into his jeans pockets, and walked over beside his mother. He looked out to where a truck pumped fuel into the plane. "What're you gonna do, Mom?" he asked.

Claire just shrugged.

Passengers were filling up the waiting section. The flight would board soon.

"Mom?" Mike asked.

"Yes?"

"If you don't go back with him, it's fine with me."

When Claire came to visit me the next time, she apologized for her obstinance the time before. "I wasn't cooperative," she said. "I was shouting. I'm sorry."

I told her apologies weren't necessary. "In fact," I said, "I felt we made great progress."

Claire told me that she had been sleeping well for the first time in months. She had been reading her Bible more frequently and praying more fervently. "The problems are still there," she said, "but I feel more in control. I think God is with me."

"Then why are you angry at God?" "Because Charles became a Christian." That had been the breakthrough. Claire had felt terrible saying it, and she had cried for an hour afterwards. But she had faced the truth and a dam had been opened up inside her, unleashing a flood of emotions. She had taken an important step toward wholeness.

From now on the sessions with Claire took on a different character. More and more we talked about the way she felt about her children, about Charles, about God. We were living more in the present. It was as if each new incident she related to me was like an article of old clothing. It was as if Claire was pulling these clothes out of the back of some closet, carefully folding them, and then boxing them to be disposed of permanently. More and more she talked about her future.

"I'm really pleased about one thing," she said. "Mike's doing better. He's got a girl friend at school. He's happier, I think—oh, once in a while he'll grow sullen again—but he's doing better. Wish I could say the same for Debbie."

"I think she was hit hardest," I said. "It may take time. Maybe a year or so."

"It touches everyone, doesn't it?"

I nodded. "Wife abuse is a family problem."

Later in the session Claire got back to her story. She told me of the decision she had made during those days she had stayed with friends in Chicago. Her mind was made up. She was going to get a divorce.

While in Chicago, the rest Claire sought melted quickly into a kind of exhaustion. She slept twelve to fourteen hours each of the three days she was there. Returning to Fargo, Claire felt weaker and more tired than before she left.

When the plane touched down Sunday morning, Claire was met right at the door of the plane by Mike.

"Father's here," he said.

"What?"

"He's waiting."

Sure enough, in the waiting area of the terminal Charles stood with his arms outstretched toward Claire.

"What do you want to do, Mom?" Mike asked.

"I don't want to see him."

But it was too late. Charles had started toward them. Charles greeted her. He wanted to know if she would come to church with him right away—right then. Claire, weak and tired, said no, but didn't resist when Charles picked up her luggage at baggage claim and loaded it into his car.

"I couldn't stop him from coming, Mom," Mike said.

Claire nodded and pressed her hand into his. "That's OK," she said. "Don't worry yourself about it. Are the girls all right?"

Mike nodded. "Yeah, everything's fine."

They rode together in Charles's Grand Prix straight to the church. Claire at first refused to go in. "I'll wait in the car."

Charles pleaded with her.

"I don't want a scene, Charles," Claire said. "You just want me to be seen with you. You want to make it look as if everything's fine."

"Not true," Charles replied quickly. He was standing outside the door on her side of the car. Mike had already gone in. "I think you'll be surprised. I've confessed to nearly everyone, honey. People know I've changed."

Claire didn't believe him. She was reminded of a similar time some eighteen years earlier when Charles had stood outside the car pleading with her to come in to talk with his mother. *How much has passed since then,* Claire thought. *And how little has changed.*

Claire and Charles argued more, Claire finally consenting to go in. By the time they found an empty pew in the back, the service was nearly over. What Claire had specifically said she did not want—a scene in church—had happened. When they entered, nearly everyone turned around and saw Charles and Claire together. Some smiled benignly, and Claire was sickened that all those people probably now believed that all was well, everything was mended. Claire could imagine the comments some would have later at home: "Wasn't it nice to see Charles with Claire today?" "It seems Claire finally came to forgive and forget." Claire grew furious. What did any of these people know of what she had been through? And how could they judge what she should or should not do?

Afterwards, while Charles was discussing something with one of the deacons, Pastor Jim Cranston made a path toward Claire. "How are you feeling?" he asked. "How was your trip?"

"I'm tired. And my trip was uneventful—blessedly uneventful."

"I'm glad to hear that." Pastor Cranston continued talking about different things pertaining to the church—the Sunday school curriculum, the new evangelism program, how he envisioned the church doubling in two years—and Claire didn't pay much attention. But one thing he said jolted her back into reality.

It came out of the clear blue: "So, what are you going to do, Claire?"

"And what did you say?" I asked.
"I don't remember," she said. "I honestly don't remember."

Claire was sitting, as usual in the naugahide recliner in my office. She had by now become a familiar fixture in that chair. I had joked with her once that I ought to retire the chair in her name. There wouldn't be too many more sessions after this one. I would miss her.

"Whatever I said," Claire went on, "it wasn't forceful. I allowed them to manipulate me."

"They?"

"Charles and the pastor. Oh, *now* I see it a little differently. Both the pastor and Charles had good intentions, I'm sure. But they did manipulate me. The pastor was "guilting" me into going back. Charles seemed so genuinely changed that it became my responsibility to make the marriage work."

"They weren't concerned about *you;* they were concerned about the marriage."

"Right." Claire sighed. It was as if my saying that had taken a load off her shoulders. More and more there were moments just like that. And I had noticed changes as a result of those moments—perhaps as a result of the therapy in general. She was more animated in the discussions, less depressed or somber. She even walked differently now—straighter, surer, more deliberately. Tears came to her less often, and Claire was more inclined to meet my gaze and hold it; she had learned to trust me with her emotions, and more important, to trust herself with them as well.

Claire had gone through a cycle of emotions common to most battered women going through the process of healing. The cycle begins with denial and progresses through anger, "bargaining," depression, and ultimately acceptance—the woman finding a sense of peace with herself and with God. For Claire, most of her eighteen years of marriage had been spent in denial. She had pretended that the abuse was not real or was in some way insignificant. When she no longer could deny that Charles was maliciously abusing her, she became angry at him. It was that anger which motivated Claire to walk out. The face-to-face meeting with the pastor and Charles and the consequences of that encounter exemplified the stage in the cycle called bargaining. And later, during the time that Claire had first come to me, she had been going through depression, characterized by gloominess, self-pity and hopelessness.

Acceptance is the fifth stage of the cycle, and the key to acceptance is found in the biblical concept of forgiveness.

It is no coincidence that whenever Jesus healed those who were sick or diseased, he also forgave their sins. It seems to me that what plagues the battered wife so very much is a combination of guilt and anger directed not only at the husband, but also at God, and perhaps in yet another way at the woman herself. For a woman to be healed, she needs to forgive. She needs to forgive God, because even though God is not to blame for her misery, she may easily perceive him to be so. She needs also to forgive herself for doing or not doing certain things which in retrospect appear to have been foolish and naive but at the time were natural reactions to a most unnatural situation. And finally she needs to forgive the man who abused her, the hardest thing to do. This step may take years; sometimes it never comes about at all.

By now Claire had "forgiven" God. She was in the process of forgiving herself. But it would be a long time before she could fully forgive Charles. Slowly, she was passing from the fourth stage, depression, into that fifth stage, acceptance. Gradually, Claire was beginning to accept herself as a human being, a woman of beauty and worth.

Nearly two months after Claire had walked out on Charles, she moved back in.

Persuaded by her pastor, charmed by her husband, and too weak and confused to put up a fight, Claire consented to a trial period during which Charles's behavior would constantly be monitored according to that list of conditions and promises drawn up that Thursday night in the pastor's study.

It would make a happier story to say that Claire moved back in with new hope and fresh feelings. But that did not happen.

Walking up the sidewalk toward the house in which so many scenes of her life had been played out, all the old emotions descended on her once again—fear, nervousness, confusion.

She was back home.

Epilogue

On a night two years and seven months later, in the foothills of western North Dakota, a small wood-frame church stood bravely against a bitter wind. The cars in the parking lot—about fifty in all—huddled against the rain. The church door was bathed in white light, and on that door hung a cross—the cross of Christ's suffering and triumph.

It was the season of Easter, a season of death and rebirth, a season of violence and resurrection. Those who drove by that night and observed the little white church from the road some 400 yards away might well have assumed that the goings-on inside were celebrations of Christ's victory over death 2000 years before.

In fact, what those passers-by were witness to was a wedding: Claire sat in the second pew from the front with her husband Charles beside her. To Claire's right sat Tricia, now fourteen, who earlier had been sick to death because her hair had gotten rained on; later she was comforted with the help of a portable hair blower in the ladies room. In the back of the church, in the narthex, one member of the bridal party —Debbie—stood nervously, preparing herself for the procession. And at the front beside the altar, Mike stood proud, awaiting his bride. He was dressed in a white tuxedo and a smile.

Of all the thoughts that tumbled through Claire's mind those moments before the wedding began, one stood out. It was contained within a single word—rebirth. In this context this day, in a humble Christian church in North Dakota, the word carried a wealth of meaning. This was of course the occasion to remember the resurrected Christ. But it was more than that. It was the time when Mike and his bride would be "reborn" into a new life together. And as Claire pondered these things she thought of her own marriage, her own family, and her own life. In a sense, all had been resurrected, all had been brought back to life.

The procession had begun to the simple sound of a guitar. Mike stood straight and watched with watery eyes as his bride, in white lace, walked up the aisle. Charles was smiling. When he turned slightly to watch the procession, his eyes met Claire's, and for a moment the two really saw each other. But it was a connection too painful to hold. Claire turned, and Charles looked straight ahead again.

Claire thought about the past two and a half years. The abuse had stopped. Not once had Charles raised his hand to her, although he raised his voice from time to time. He still became angry, but he was careful now not to direct his rage at Claire. He had learned to be genuinely considerate of her. The "contract" he and the pastor had drawn up was one he lived up to—to the letter. In a way this bothered Claire—she wished his sense of responsibility toward her could be more spontaneous—but then she couldn't really complain.

Not only that, but Charles had become a good father, working especially hard to regain Mike's trust. And now as Mike stood up front, a tall, strong specimen of a man, Charles was proud; perhaps it was in Mike that a little of Charles could be reborn. On more than one occasion Claire would see Mike and Charles exchange glances—evidence of a warm relationship. For these and other things Claire was grateful.

There was no doubt that Charles had changed. Claire wasn't sure at first how genuine his conversion had been, but was sure now. Claire felt that maybe over time Charles had come to believe in that which he had originally used as a device to secure his wife's return. And it was this shared belief in Christ which now, more than any other thing, held the couple together.

The pastor spoke: "We are gathered here today to join together this man and this woman in holy matrimony." Mike and his young bride were kneeling together at the altar.

Tricia, sitting beside Claire, brushed the hair from her face with her hand and crossed her legs. She was becoming a woman. Fortunately—and, oh, how Claire thanked God for this night after night—Tricia had never been touched by the abuse.

Debbie had not been so lucky. Her depression had lasted nearly eighteen months. Even now she was not out of it. In high school she had struggled—with her sense of worth, her identity, with Christianity. She had for a time gotten involved with a bad crowd of kids. In the past few months, however, she had improved. She was going to church with the family again. She planned to start college in September. Charles had insisted. "I'll pay for it," he had said.

The pastor was speaking about the spiritual nature of marriage. "Marriage is a privilege," he was saying, "and the Bible tells us it involves responsibilities. We often speak of the verse in Ephesians which tells wives to submit to their husbands. Less often do we read the verse which tells husbands to love their wives. Marriage is a relationship of mutual giving, not individuals taking."

Claire knew Mike would give all he had to his wife. She was certain he loved his bride and would love her the rest of his life. Several days earlier he had said something very interesting. Claire and Mike had been alone together working out some arrangements for the rehearsal dinner. During a quiet moment Claire had asked, "Does it ever hurt any more?"

"But *you* were the one who was hurt," he said.

"So were you. I know. I'm your mother."

Mike laughed. "Yeah, I keep forgetting that."

"So," Claire persisted, "does it still hurt?"

Mike thought a moment. "Once in a while," he said. "It's like that old football injury of mine—you know, when I was spiked in the side. It's healed, sure, but every so often it'll flare up. I'll feel a twinge."

"The pain never really goes away, does it?"

Mike shook his head. "But you know, Mom," he said. "I'm gonna make a good husband." He smiled.

Claire hugged him. She whispered, "I know you will. You know too much to be able to hurt her."

Now at the front of the church Mike was saying his vows. The couple had written their own. Mike had spent long hours, Claire knew, perfecting what he would say. It was important to him. Vows, promises, contracts—Claire's life had been filled with them all broken—but she knew that whatever Mike would say, whatever he would commit himself to, he would do.

So this was the good that came out of it all; here was the treasure salvaged from the wreck of Claire's life. In Mike, Claire's life would find purpose, meaning, value. In his marriage, her marriage would be granted some worth after all.

The pastor quoted a Scripture verse: "Old things are passed away; behold, all things have become new." *Maybe so,* Claire thought. *But....*

Though Charles had changed, though the children had gotten better, though it seemed now that Claire had survived, her past was ever present. Eighteen years of abuse could not be erased overnight, nor in months or even years. Even in a marriage resurrected by the power and grace of God the wounds were still evident. Mike had gotten it right—from time to time the pain still flared up.

Love was hard coming between Claire and Charles. Perhaps the best that could be said was that she and Charles had learned to be friends. They lived in a state of peaceful coexistence. But still, after two and a half years of peace, Claire tensed up whenever Charles raised his voice or got the least bit angry. Claire had become conditioned to feel that way. And when Claire tensed up or got upset, that would disturb Charles. He would become fearful again that she would leave him. So even now, although much had improved, they walked on eggshells. Each person's feeble and tentative expression of love toward the other—a glance, a touch, a kind word, a sudden urge to kiss—would miss by mere minutes or seconds the other's similar moods and would fall into the vacuum between them.

The wedding was nearly over. The young couple up front had exchanged rings and now a kiss. *How could love once have been so easy?* Claire thought. *Is that still possible with Charles?*

The pastor delivered a final exhortation. "God is at work here," he said, and he could have been referring as much to that weary couple in the second pew as well as to the young couple kneeling up front. "Let us help this marriage to grow in the Lord. Let us grant the nurture and care that it will require. At times the road will be hard. But with God's grace, love will abound."

In the second pew from the front Charles reached for Claire's hand. And for once it was there, waiting. Together they clasped hands and watched as their son and his bride walked down the aisle together.

Appendix One
Christian Women and Abuse

Does wife abuse occur in Christian homes?

It shocks us to think that it does. Our reaction might be similar to Claire's reaction after she was first beaten by Charles—one of denial. We might think, "It can't happen often," or "It must happen only to Christians who aren't strong in the faith." Unfortunately, there is evidence that wife abuse does occur in Christian homes, that Christian husbands beat Christian wives, and that sometimes the abusers are clergymen.

Maxine Hoffman, in an article in the *Pentecostal Evangel*, writes: "Statistics indicate that one of two women, Christian or otherwise, is battered at some time during her life." Her figures are no doubt based on the research by Straus, Gelles, and Steinmetz which shows that women from *all* socio-economic and religious levels are abused at similar rates of occurrence. In fact, these researchers suggest in their book *Behind Closed Doors* that in some cases religious orientation actually aggravates the problem.

Probably the most frequent situation is one in which the woman is a Christian and the husband is not. Lenore Walker found in her study of wife abuse that some "women indicated they no longer practiced their religion, because giving it up eliminated a point of conflict with their batterer."

Statistics detailing the frequency of wife abuse among Christians just do not exist. Even if they did, they probably would not be accurate; neither husbands nor wives would be inclined to admit to it. We hear more about the problem of wife abuse in Christian homes from Christian counselors and pastors who find this problem growing at an alarming rate. Stories like Claire's are common. Lucille Travis, in her article "Are There Battered Women in Your Pews?" (*Eternity*, November 1981), tells of a pastor who sat all night facing an angry husband with a gun. "Another pastor," she writes, "with his wife, had opened the parsonage door to a woman from their congregation, beaten and raped by her drunken husband and his friends."

One of the most helpful books on wife abuse is *Conjugal Crime* by Terry Davidson. She relates her own story of growing up in a home in which her father beat her mother. Her father was a Christian minister. At church he was a man of God; at home he was brutal, often exploding in a tirade of verbal and physical abuse before or after saying grace at the dinner table. Davidson's story is not the only case of clergy abuse. Counselors who work with child and spouse abuse cases find that clergymen are guilty of battering their wives and children more often than we would like to believe.

Maxine Hoffman sums it up: "There is a great deal of battering happening in Christian marriages, even in our churches, right under our noses."

The evidence is clear and chilling: wife abuse really does happen in the Christian home.

Special Problems

Claire's story forces us to think about the special problems abused Christians face. If you are a Christian, you quite possibly have been raised in a church culture in which your responsibility to your spouse and family has been stressed again and again from the pulpit. You have traditional values, and you believe these values important to the fabric of the family as well as society. You no doubt hold a high and special view of marriage. And not least of all, you believe that Jesus Christ can and does change lives. For you—whether you have a friend who has been abused or are a victim yourself—wife abuse poses special problems that the non-Christian woman does not face.

Abuse literature and feminism. One problem may be that much of the secular advice about wifebeating written in books and magazines has a decided feminist bias. Frankly, the subject of the battered woman is a persuasive argument for feminism; it testifies to the fact that abusive men do dominate and brutalize women. Claire's story, although not intended as a defense of feminism, can't help but bear witness to the power a husband can gain over his wife. *It happens*—and insofar as secular books and magazine articles make us aware of this, they can be helpful. Also, these various publications agree on one important point: that women are significant persons. This is not only good advice for the battered woman, but it is sound biblical advice as well.

Much of what you may read will be helpful. But ultimately wife abuse literature written from a feminist perspective does not understand the Christian woman. It treats marriage as dispensable; the Christian woman does not. It tends to suggest that homemaking is an inferior role in life; the Christian woman, though she may even have a prosperous career, disagrees—she feels that raising a family and making a home is an equally valid and worthy calling. Wife abuse literature often adopts a cynical, negative attitude toward Christianity, seeing it as the historical cause for the oppression of women. The Christian woman understands that throughout history this has sometimes been true, but that it is not in keeping with the teaching and example of Jesus Christ.

If you are seeking help for a friend or for yourself, you may find some in the available published material on wife abuse, but you may also be disappointed. You may not find there any sympathy for your spiritual beliefs; your special needs may not be adequately addressed.

The problem of submission. Probably the central dilemma for Christian women caught in marital abuse is how to fulfill the biblical teaching on submission. (This is a good example of how secular advice to the battered woman so often fails. Most of the books on wifebeating treat submission briefly and condescendingly; they don't understand that submission is an important part of the way millions of women think about their families and homes.)

Of course, in the Christian community submission has been a controversial subject in recent years. One look inside a Christian bookstore at all the books on marriage and submission testifies to how this debate rages on. Not only has submission been argued pro and con, but endless varieties of the submission teaching have been proposed. In other words, the argument has become sophisticated and complex.

The authors of this book feel that it isn't in the interest of the abused wife for us to assert our own personal views on submission. We don't see any reason to jump into the fray. But an important point must be made concerning the dangers of the submission teaching when it is applied to wife abuse.

Our concern is for those abused Christian women who take the submission teaching to an extreme, even when their lives may be in danger. This, we believe, is at odds with the biblical teaching of the sanctity of life and the value that Jesus Christ himself attributed to women. You cannot read the Gospels without sensing the compassion Christ felt toward women, women who often found themselves in places of subservience and abuse. Jesus said, "The Spirit of the Lord . . . has sent me . . . to set at liberty those who are oppressed" (Luke 4:16-20). When Jesus spoke to the woman taken in adultery, he said, "Where are those thine accusers? hath no man condemned thee? . . . Neither do I condemn thee: go, and sin no more" (John 8:10, 11, KJV). Susan Thistlewaite writes in *Christianity and Crisis,* "In the life of Jesus of Nazareth, the character of God is revealed as one who sides with the oppressed, those unfairly treated in society, and whose judgment is on those who oppress, who misuse others for their own selfish ends."

The Bible does not teach that a woman should submit to abuse and battering. If you are an abused Christian woman, know that God does not want you to suffer. Jesus truly loves you. He values your life. He wants you alive—safe and free from violence.

The problem of divorce. The *St. Paul Dispatch* reports on one wife who had been battered by her husband for many years.

She was a Christian and held strong convictions concerning the sanctity of marriage. But she could take just so much physical abuse. She went to her pastor for help. She said she didn't believe in divorce, but that her life was in danger. She wanted to move out.

The minister didn't understand the problem. He said that she had entered into a sacred union. He stressed that it would be wrong for her to leave the home. He said that if she left the home, she probably would find it hard to return and would eventually seek a divorce. He implied that if she walked out she would be a bad wife and a home-wrecker.

Many Christians believe, as this abused wife and this minister did, that divorce is unacceptable for Christians. The biblical teaching about divorce is specific and authoritative, coming as it does straight from the lips of Christ. As happened in this case, some abused Christians who feel strongly about the divorce teaching may discourage themselves or be discouraged by well-meaning friends and professionals from leaving their husbands, getting out of the home, and seeking shelter.

The authors of this book also believe strongly in the sanctity of marriage. We feel that Christians' attitudes toward divorce have become increasingly liberalized in recent years, yielding tragic results. Nevertheless, we also understand Christ's teaching that divorce is permissible in the case of infidelity (Matt. 5:32), and we believe that the threat of physical injury or death to a Christian woman is certainly even more serious than adultery. We believe the abused Christian wife is justified in protecting herself and separating from her abusing husband; sometimes divorce may be the only way that a battered woman can secure freedom from violence and terror.

That is our opinion. Others will take a stricter view of the divorce teaching, believing that even a case of wife abuse does not justify divorce. To the abused Christians who hold this view, we would suggest that moving out of the home is not tantamount to seeking a divorce. An abused woman whose life is in danger must flee. And she can make any number of choices once she steps out of the home. Our concern is to see her take that first step.

If you are an abused woman, or if you have a friend who is

being abused, you might want to think about what Terry Davidson writes in *Conjugal Crime:* "[You must] realize that [he] will never change unless he gets psychological help or is intimidated into nonviolence by exposure and punishment." The only way you can help your husband is by forcing him to recognize the serious consequences of what he has done. Ironically, it may take the threat of divorce to bring him to this point.

The salvation syndrome. This may best be illustrated by Claire's own story: As a teenage girl she felt sorry for Charles. She felt she could help him find himself. She was a Christian; he was not. Claire felt that with time and understanding Charles might come to Christ. She married him.

That is the "salvation syndrome." Many Christian wives possess this same spiritual sense of responsibility for their non-Christian husbands. A Christian woman may see herself as her non-Christian husband's rescuer, enabler, perfecter, and ultimately even his savior. This last role—"savior"—may be the one the abused Christian woman emphasizes: She may feel, mistakenly, that if he becomes saved the abuse will stop and the problem will be solved.

Sometimes the incentive for the salvation syndrome comes not from the woman herself but from her pastor or church. Lenore Walker notes that in her survey "some women told stories in which their religious adviser suggested they pray for guidance, become better women, and go home and help their husbands 'become more spiritual and find the Lord.' Needless to say, these women did not have time to wait for their husbands to 'find the Lord' while they continued to receive brutal beatings."

There are several problems with the salvation syndrome, and if you are an abused Christian wife or if you have a friend who is abused, you should be aware of them. Most seriously, of course, is that it is a delusion. An abused woman who feels she can be her husband's rescuer and savior is not facing reality; she doesn't understand the antagonistic relationship she is in. It is also true that the salvation syndrome is dangerous: it may be interpreted by the abuser as a threat and lead to further violence. As Lenore Walker points out, while the wife is waiting for her husband to find the Lord she may be beaten severely.

But probably the biggest problem with this "Messianic complex" is that it presumes to do the work of God. In thinking of herself as rescuer or enabler or perfecter or savior, the woman may forget God's omnipotence and infinite ability to change people and circumstances—with or without her help. In fact, it may cause her to overlook the possibility that it may be precisely her decision to leave her husband that God uses to move him toward healing, change, and ultimately salvation.

Getting Out

If you are an abused wife, what should you do? What steps should you take to protect yourself? What is an appropriate Christian response to the situation?

No one can make your decisions for you. You are an individual in a unique situation. There are many variables in your life and marriage, and you may be the only one who truly knows what those variables are. You have to make your own choices.

Still, there is some advice we can give you. The following ten steps have been gleaned from various resources on the subject of wife abuse. We think this is a responsible, cautious, self-protective approach.

1. Pray. Communication with God is the first and most important step for the abused Christian woman. James, the brother of Jesus, writes in his epistle (5:13, RSV), "Is anyone among you suffering? Let him pray."

God has the power to deliver the abused woman from her torment. But she must realize that God wants her to pray to him not just because she wants something, not just because she's suddenly desperate, not just when she suddenly needs a miracle worked, but simply because she loves him. God cherishes that relationship with her, and he wants her to feel the same way.

Some abused Christian women have been praying for a long time. They wonder how long they'll have to endure before God will do something miraculous. But maybe they don't understand or accept their own responsibility. Maybe God wants them to *act,* to take care of themselves, to make decisions. Perhaps God *will* work miracles—but in his perfect timing and in tandem with a child of his who is willing to work and act too.

God, of course, *can* work miracles. But that's not the sole purpose of prayer. Whether God works a miracle or not, the abused woman should cherish her prayer life for the renewed and deepened contact it provides with her God and Savior.

2. If your life is threatened, leave the home. Threats of violence or murder are not uncommon in wife abuse cases. Such threats are made in two ways—verbally, and by means of physical abuse so severe that it carries the woman to the brink of death. However the threat of murder is conveyed, the abused woman should as soon as possible seek shelter from her abuser.

Sometimes the batterer threatens, "If you leave me, I'll find you and kill you!" This is often not an empty threat. However, a woman should not be intimidated into staying. Yes, there is danger if she should leave, but there is even more danger should she stay. The advice given by all experts is, "Get out!" Ways can be found to protect an abused woman from her rampaging husband if she is under others' care. But by staying in the home, she remains completely vulnerable.

3. Let others know about the problem. When a woman has been abused for some time, never saying anything to anyone about it, *and then suddenly leaves the home,* she will have trouble convincing others that abuse actually occurred. Wife abuse authorities advise women to "build a case" for herself by informing friends and relatives about what is happening long before the decision is made to leave the home. It is helpful to have a doctor's statement confirming the extent of the abuse, and a pastor, minister, or priest should be informed as well. All of this may be done discreetly, of course, but it nevertheless should be done.

4. Communicate your anger to your husband. Though it sounds incredible, sometimes the batterer does not understand why his wife has left him. With some men, because of their personal and cultural backgrounds, wife abuse is thought to be legitimate, a normal part of what they perceive to be the sovereignty of the husband. To other men the consequences of their actions have never been made clear. The abused wife should make sure that her husband understands that what he is doing is wrong. She should inform him what the consequences will be if he continues.

5. *Determine what it will take to cause you to leave your husband, and plan ahead so that you'll be prepared if that day comes.* In other words, the abused woman needs to draw the line somewhere. If the batterer steps beyond that line, the abused woman should make good on her commitment to leave.

Ahead of time the battered wife should keep a mental list of things that need to be cared for in the event that she would leave the home. She should consider her financial situation (Does she have a separate checking account?), her opportunities for alternative shelter (Where will she stay?), and how best to care for the children (Are they also in danger? What will least disrupt their lives?).

6. *If physical abuse occurs a third time, leave the home.* The authors of this book agree that three occasions of physical abuse constitutes a pattern. Any fewer than that and it will be hard for a woman to convince others of the problem. We refer to point 3: It is important for the abused woman to build her case with the people around her. And we hasten to restate point 2: If the abuse is life-threatening—even if it is the first occasion—the woman should immediately seek protection and shelter.

7. *In finding an alternative place to live, make sure that it is safe from the abuser.* Langley and Levy, in their book *Wife Beating: The Silent Crisis,* tell the true story of Tracy, an abused wife who had left her husband and was living with her mother. Her husband Tom discovered where she was staying and telephoned her at night, threatening her. He also came to the house, pushed past Tracy's mother, and punched Tracy in the stomach and chest. When he had left, Tracy called the police and filed a complaint. Later, although a warrant was issued, he was never picked up. (The police prefer not to get involved in domestic disturbances.) One night Tom came to the house again. Again he shoved aside Tracy's mother. This

time he chased Tracy upstairs into the bedroom, threatening her above the screams of the two women. Tracy pulled out a hand gun and shot her husband dead.

This is told not for the purpose of frightening anyone. It illustrates two important points about wife abuse. In the first place, women can't always count on the law enforcement system to protect them. Second, it is essential that a woman find shelter safe from the menace of the batterer.

It is tempting to say that cases like Tracy's are rare, but in fact they are more common than we might think—or want to think. The abused woman should learn a lesson from this: once she is outside the home, her husband will very likely try to locate her and may try to meet her personally. His purposes may be benign (he may just want to apologize and ask for forgiveness) or they may be violent.

There are no hard and fast rules. Each situation is different. Each abused woman will have to determine the true intentions of her husband. She should indeed be open to the possibility of his honest desire to change, to talk, to be counseled, to win her back. At the same time she needs to be aware of the realities of certain wife abuse cases. Her husband's intentions may not be so pure.

We'd like to think that such a sordid scene as happened at Tracy's mother's house that night could not happen to Christians. But it can. It *has* happened. And we are reminded that many Christian women are married to husbands who do not share their faith or any of the principles of Scripture, men whose lives are and always have been steeped in violence.

Those who are wise will try to prevent the occurrence of violence and seek shelter in a place that is secure.

8. Go to a doctor. The abused woman needs immediate medical attention. This not only cares for a woman's injuries, some of which may be internal and more serious than bruises or cuts, but it also gets professional verification that abuse has occurred.

9. Seek a support community. The abused woman needs emotional and psychological support. For the Christian woman this support may or may not come from the church. (As we shall see later, the church may not understand the problem of wife abuse.) If the church community will not lend help and understanding, the abused woman needs to establish a regular contact with two or three friends who will help her through this very difficult time in her life.

10. Find a Christian counselor. Even when the abused wife has found safety in a shelter outside the home, and even after her bruises have healed, she still has a long road to travel. She needs constant counseling by a professional, not just a friend. For the Christian woman it is important that this counselor be a Christian who understands wife abuse.

The abused woman should not become discouraged in her counseling progress. Above all, she should not shop around for better counselors. Psychological healing takes time; rapport between the counselor and the client also takes time to develop properly. The abused Christian woman should be patient and give God a chance to work through his servants.

Consulting the Pastor

The battered wife may be surprised to find that her pastor, minister, or priest may not be equipped to give her the kind of support and help that she is looking for.

In one informal survey of clergymen, there were three categories of response to wife abuse:

1. Those who are naive concerning wife abuse and other contemporary family problems.
2. Those who are aware, but who believe that wife abuse is best dealt with by the wife remaining home, enduring the abuse, and seeking pastoral counseling for herself and her husband.
3. Those who believe the problem cannot be worked out within the home and who encourage the wife to leave her husband, even only temporarily.

Fortunately, because seminaries and Bible schools have developed curriculum that stresses the modern problems of wife and child abuse, alcoholism, and drug addiction, the number of clergymen who fall into the first category seems to be diminishing. Still there are stories of ignorance: Lucille Travis, in *Eternity* magazine, writes of one pastor who was contacted by one of the men in his church. This man's wife had left the home, claiming to have been beaten and seeking refuge in a local wife abuse shelter. The pastor called her at the shelter and threatened excommunication if she were not at home by eight in the morning.

Most clergymen, however, are more reasonable. Many are troubled by the problem of wife abuse in their churches. They are aware, from counseling experiences, that the epidemic has afflicted Christians as well as non-Christians. These pastors, ministers, and priests feel everything should be done to keep families and marriages intact. An abused Christian wife is likely to hear from such a person that it is her responsibility to her husband and her marriage to remain in the home and to seek solutions from the inside. She is likely to be warned that once she steps outside the home—once she leaves her husband—it will be difficult to return. These clergymen—those that fall into the second category—are likely to advise a woman to find out what she may be doing to set her husband off, the implication being that in some way the abuse may be her fault.

Fewer clergymen fall into the third category: those who believe that wife abuse cannot be remedied from within the home. Some of these maintain a low view of marriage, feeling that the marriage bond is dispensable. But many others hold to a high view of marriage while at the same time understanding the realities of wife abuse. They realize something important: that in many cases the life of the woman is being threatened monthly, weekly, and sometimes daily. They feel that the issue is not only the survival of a marriage, but also the survival of a human being, a woman who suffers at the hand of a man who can be brutal and irrational.

Abused women and friends of abused women should also keep in mind that most church leaders are male; they may not be able to fully sympathize with the battered wife; they may at heart be unaware of the particular terrors of living in the midst of domestic violence.

What should the abused woman do then? Well, the pastor, minister, or priest *should* be consulted. In many cases the advice and spiritual help that a clergyman provides will be of enormous benefit. But the abused wife looking for a shoulder to cry on should not be surprised to find something of a cold shoulder instead.

What should clergymen do to improve their awareness of the wife abuse problem? First, they should not underestimate or disbelieve the claims of anyone complaining of abuse; the problem is too widespread for that kind of a response. Second, they should consult some of the popular women's magazines (*Redbook, Good Housekeeping, Ladies Home Journal,* to name a few), which have for years spoken about the problem of abuse in the family. Such contact with the woman's perspective of the problem will no doubt help as well. Finally, clergymen should preach that abuse of women and children is clearly unbiblical.

Going Before the Church

Most abused women, like Claire, are afraid to tell church members about their problems at home. There is good reason for this. Most churches are not prepared physically, emotionally, or spiritually to deal with wife abuse. It's not the fault of the congregation. Many reading this book are church members and understand well that marital problems are touchy topics, that wife abuse is unpleasant and frightening, and that sometimes church involvement in a marriage can be messy and may hurt more than help. Church people are understandably reluctant to involve themselves too deeply in the epidemic of wife abuse.

Still, isn't it part of the Christian's responsibility to help those who hurt? And isn't it the church's responsibility to care for the members of the body? *The Living Bible* says that we in the church "have been given freedom . . . to love and serve each other" (Gal. 5:13). And Christ's statement in Matthew 25:35 (TLB)—"When you refused to help the least of these my brothers, you were refusing help to me"—hauntingly presents the church's duty to care for those in need. Despite the unsavoriness of the subject and despite the church's qualms about "getting involved" in the mire of bad marital relationships, it remains the church's Christian responsibility to deal with the problem of wife abuse, to seek its prevention, and to extend its arms to those abused wives in its pews.

There are stories of churches' positive action, and these offer promise and hope to the battered woman. One such story concerns a woman we shall call Karen.

Although she was a Sunday school teacher, Karen felt aloof and distant from other church members. She felt incapable of telling anyone that her husband was abusing her. But one night her husband attacked her. Karen sang in church the next day in spite of the pain in her bruised muscles. It was a classic communications gap: Karen couldn't tell about the abuse, and the congregation wasn't warm enough or close enough to her to suspect anything was wrong. "I desperately needed people to figure out that I was hurting," Karen says now. "To me, the crux of why abused women go on and on covering up is because no one is taking the time to get to know them."

Karen switched churches. This new congregation opened its arms to her, even though it was still quite a while before anyone knew of the abuse. People called Karen and asked her to dinner or to a special church function. They won her friendship, and she began to open up to them.

Later Karen's husband left her, and she needed support more than ever. She got it. Soon Karen was able to tell a few close friends what had happened. They responded beautifully, helping her, caring for her, and leading her through the process of healing.

This is how a church should handle the battered women in its sanctuary. Unfortunately, such stories are rare. The abused wife cannot count on receiving help from the church. It may happen, but then again it may not. Karen spent seven years in a church which was oblivious to her need before she found a church that cared.

If you are an abused woman or if you have a friend who is, you might benefit from the following advice about sharing with others in the Body of Christ. First, remember that churches are made up of people, and people, unfortunately, aren't perfect. They may seem unaware of your pain. Do not overlook the possibility that many of them may be in pain too. Reaching out to others may be a way of finding help for yourself. Second, do take that daring step and share your need with one or two close church friends. It may open a considerable source of love and compassion you never thought existed. Third, be discreet. The whole church needn't be involved. Just a few close friends. They will serve as a buffer for you. They will tell others just enough to indicate that you are hurting and need love and prayer; at the same time they will help protect your privacy. Finally, as we've stated, pray. Pray for your own healing, sure, but don't forget those close church friends and confidantes have hurts too.

Seeking Shelter

Shelters for women seeking comfort, support, safety, and refuge have emerged in the past decade as one alternative for the abused woman. If you are abused or have a friend who is a victim of abuse, and especially if you have no other place to turn—no friends, relatives, co-workers who will help you or who can provide shelter—you may wish to consider staying for a time at a wife abuse shelter.

There are more than 185 shelters and nearly 140 other "service providers," as Jennifer Baker Fleming labels them (services and programs) for the battered woman in the United States. Unfortunately, these shelters are almost always full. The State of Minnesota, which has four times as many shelters as other states (a total of fourteen), turned away 2,900 women (1979 figures) for lack of space. Only 30 percent of those who needed shelter were able to find it.

The abused Christian woman should keep in mind that most of these shelters have no religious affiliation, and a lot of them have a heavy feminist orientation. Once inside, one is likely to receive the sort of counsel that advises in favor of a divorce.

It may be that the abused Christian woman would do better to seek shelter from her friends in the church. Some churches have gone so far as to set up abuse centers, but these are few.

In short, the picture for battered women seeking shelter is a rather bleak one, although in the right place and in the right circumstances shelter might be available.

Conclusion

This brief chapter does not pretend to be a handbook for battered women. It is meant to be an overview of the special needs and problems that abused *Christian* women have. Far more detailed information on the problem of wife abuse in general can be found at the library or in the bookstore. Some of these books are listed following this chapter. Many of these books will provide helpful information on such matters as the law and the courts, wife abuse and law enforcement, and treatment for the batterer.

The abused Christian woman has a hard road ahead. Not only does she have to face the forest of fears inherent in wife abuse, but she also has to sort through the thickets of doctrine and religious conviction that are so much a part of her identity. It is a most difficult task, and while she attempts it she is afflicted by wildly fluctuating emotions, low self-esteem, and intense loneliness. It is an arduous journey.

But just as her Christian background poses special problems and unique difficulties, so it offers special comfort and unique solace. For God is real. And he holds those who suffer close to his heart. The Apostle Peter wrote, "He cares for you." Yes. It is in Christ that we find deliverance, all of us—the poor, the lonely, the heartbroken, the abused. We find shelter in Christ.

Appendix Two
Help from Books

Reading about wife abuse is not, in itself, a solution for the battered woman. The abused wife needs personal contact, counsel, and friendship. These are things that books can't provide.

But what books can do is to tell people that the problem of abuse exists in alarming proportions in our society. Books can increase our knowledge about domestic violence; and from knowledge may emerge ideas and programs, preventions and cures. More than anything, books offer the battered wife a new perspective about herself and about her world. They tell her that she is not alone.

Much has been written about wife abuse; little has come from a Christian perspective. It may be that religious publishers will awaken to the need in this area. One Christian book that speaks to the issue is *Coping with Abuse in the Family* by Wesley R. Monfalcone (Westminster). You won't find here an in-depth treatment of the wife abuse issue, but you will find that Mr. Monfalcone writes in a compassionate style. He argues persuasively that wife abuse is an extreme, violent form of the subtle abuses that we all use on each other every day. It suggests that we all are guilty of abusing others—we all have sinned.

Another book that may be helpful is not about the battered

woman, but something closely related—the problem of pain. Philip Yancey's brief paperback, *Where Is God When It Hurts?* (Zondervan/Campus Life Books) has in five short years become a small classic. We recommend it highly.

For facts and figures about the wife abuse phenomenon *Behind Closed Doors: Violence in the American Family* by Straus, Gelles, and Steinmetz is the pioneer research in the field. It will be of interest mainly to those who are interested in the sociological nature of the problem. The book is published by Anchor Books/Doubleday.

The classic on the subject is *Battered Wives* by Del Martin (Pocket Books). Much has been written about wife abuse since its release in 1976, but it remains a solid overview and provides a detailed listing and description of shelters and women's centers. An even more extensive listing of programs and services can be found in *Stopping Wife Abuse* by Jennifer Baker Fleming (Anchor Press/Doubleday). Fleming's book is especially helpful in explaining the legal problems a battered wife is likely to face. *Wife Beating: The Silent Crisis* by Langley and Levy (Pocket Books) is interesting primarily for its four chapter-long case studies, written succinctly and powerfully. Reading the true stories of Anne, Maria, Karen, and Tracy brings the problem of abuse out of the realm of statistics and into the world of emotions. Lenore Walker's *The Battered Woman* (Harper Colophon), is especially good when it speaks of "learned helplessness"—the state abused women find themselves in which makes them feel powerless to change their situations—and when it lists the various myths (twenty-one in all) of wife abuse. Fascinating reading, and sure to help the abused woman see herself more clearly. Finally, Terry Davidson's *Conjugal Crime* is interesting particularly because it recounts, in chapter 7, the story of Terry's father, a minister and a wife beater. The author also writes vividly of the various emotions an abused woman feels in a section called "How Does It Feel to Be Beaten?"

There are many more books on the battered wife, but these are among the best. For further reading, consult the bibliographies in *Behind Closed Doors* and *Wife Beating: The Silent Crisis*. The former lists primarily articles in journals and magazines.